Identity Diet

Eight Guiding Principles for Identity Protection

Henry Bagdasarian

iUniverse, Inc.
New York Bloomington

Identity Diet™
Eight Guiding Principles for Identity Protection

iUniverse books may be ordered through booksellers or by contacting:

iUniverse
1663 Liberty Drive
Bloomington, IN 47403
www.iuniverse.com
1-800-Authors (1-800-288-4677)

ISBN: 978-1-4502-3867-0 (sc)
ISBN: 978-1-4502-3869-4 (dj)
ISBN: 978-1-4502-3868-7 (ebook)

Library of Congress Control Number: 2010908932

Printed in the United States of America

iUniverse rev. date: 06/24/2010

Table of Contents

Dedication

I dedicate my first book to my wife Eileen, my daughter Paulina, my son Daniel and all my dear friends, readers and clients. I am also deeply grateful to god as well as all past and current teachers, philosophers, creative thinkers and writers whose wisdom and guidance I have studied over the years and continue to apply in my own life for continued personal growth. They have all been a collective source of inspiration and motivation for me during my self discovery period, in which I defined my life purpose and identified my passionate desires, natural talents and the value I can provide to the society. I also discovered that life seems to reward most those who dare to dream big, search and find their natural talents early on, and passionately pursue their deepest desires to completion regardless of all external opinions which have no value except the value we decide to give them.

Henry Bagdasarian

Preface

Although this is a book about identity protection for consumers, I have noticed many similarities between food and credit products in terms of the root causes and consequences of their over consumption which I propose we analyze before discussing identity theft. Every one agrees that consumer obesity or the excess fat weight is on the rise and its root cause has been identified to be health mismanagement including excessive consumption of junk food. Similarly, identity mismanagement including over consumption of credit products and excessive sharing of personal information have led to identity obesity with identity theft and fraud consequences. Although some businesses are also identity obese by excessively collecting, retaining and sharing their customer information and sometimes fail to properly protect the private information of their customers, the focus of this book is to help consumers protect their identities against identity theft and fraud.

I have been helping businesses within financial services and health insurance industries protect consumer information for many years while working as Chief Information Security Officer (CISO) and Chief Privacy Officer (CPO). Ever since I started researching and writing about identity theft, I have proposed many new concepts, solutions, and industry terms to address the root cause of identity theft which I consider to be identity obesity. I believe that as excess consumption of junk food leads to obesity or excess fat weight, the excess and inappropriate collection, retention and sharing of personal information lead to identity obesity placing consumers at a higher risk of identity theft and fraud, especially, consumers who lack awareness and education to properly protect their identities. As such, the Identity Diet ™ concept was born out of my belief that consumers must develop and act upon a customized identity protection plan to reduce their identity theft risks. Such plan helps consumers identify their unique identity theft risks and implement appropriate solutions for their lifestyle including a conscious change in behavior, purchase of automated services available in the market, as well as activation of account notification features offered by the banks and other affiliated organizations.

Recently, my conclusion about the root cause of identity theft was further reinforced as I was watching a paid health program on TV. I observed how food and credit products are similar to each other with respect to their marketing campaigns and undesired consequences when over consumed. I asked myself, why do consumers continue to become identity obese while they lack the necessary knowledge to protect their identities against the increasing risk of theft, fraud and disclosure? I answered my own question with another question which is; why do consumers continue to excessively consume junk food and become obese while they know the dangers of obesity? It occurred to me that maybe aggressive marketing techniques and lack of awareness may be responsible for the epidemic in both areas. The return on advertising investment must be lucrative enough for companies to spend millions of dollars on ad campaigns and sell consumers these products while knowing that consumer lack of awareness regarding over consumption risks will push sales upward. As consumers continue to over consume these products and face the devastating consequences, companies come to their rescue by offering other products such as diet and debt consolidation programs to resolve the problems. Just pay more attention to the infomercials you see on TV and other marketing outlets; what categories of advertisements do you normally see the most? I normally see food and loan advertisings, then I also see diet, exercise and debt management programs. Some companies are even smarter and combine both categories into one like foods that help you lose weight or credit cards that come with the best protection against identity theft. Well, I think that if we consume a healthy dose of food or credit products, we won't need to lose weight or consolidate debt. We need both food and credit to have a balanced and healthy life in today's society, but as individuals, we have to define what that dose is for us because no one else can or will properly define the limit for us. The old marketing system which advocated creating problems and then offering help to fix the problems has evolved and suggests that consumers pay for creating the problems and the solutions. I hope you get the idea but the immediate similarities that came to my mind as I was watching the TV program are listed below:

1. Excess food and credit are both bad for us because they lead to serious problems. Excess food kills people and excess debt destroys families. There is no doubt that excess weight as well as high number of bankruptcies and identity fraud cases are the results of over consumption of food and credit products which have reached dangerously high levels.

2. Both food and credit are big businesses. Again, by just looking at the number of infomercials, TV programs and other advertisings, I can only guess that food and credit are big businesses. Individuals are encouraged to consume more of food and credit products and as they do that, face the serious consequences that come with the over consumption of these products.

3. Food and credit are both addictive because we tend to over consume both of them. Unless consumers are suicidal, I don't think they would excessively consume products that kill and/or destroy lives unless these products were addictive in nature and designed to make us consume more of them. Some examples of addictive products are junk foods, alcohol, cigarettes and lines of credit. Although, we know that excess food and credit consumption lead to increased weight, unmanageable debt and identity fraud, we continue to consume more of them because these products and their marketing campaigns are designed to make us consume more of them.

4. Food and credit related products exist in abundance. They are some of the most competitive categories offered to consumers and their unwanted consequences have also been more apparent in recent years. The negative results of credit over consumption include identity fraud, bankruptcies, foreclosures, and low credit

scores for which there are solutions like, credit report monitoring, refinancing, debt consolidation, and credit score improvement programs. Did you know that some credit card companies that offer credit cards also sell credit-monitoring services to help consumers detect identity theft? Do you think that our risk of credit fraud increases with each additional credit card in our pockets? You can decide for yourself.

5. Companies that sell food and credit products won't tell consumers how much they should consume while they encourage them to consume more of their products, and won't come to their rescue when consumers face the consequences of over consumption. Some companies may only think about quick increases in revenue and depend on people's addictive behaviors to achieve their goals. The loss of consumer confidence is less of a concern in these cases because companies rely on their advertising and the addictive aspect of their products to push sales upward.

6. There are plenty of advertising and professional help to resolve the consequences of excess credit and food consumption. Problems in both areas create billions of dollars in revenue for companies that come to our rescue by offering diet, exercise, debt consolidation, bankruptcy filings, and identity theft protection services and products.

In summary, I made this comparison to show you that we can become obese in all areas of our lives if we do not follow a managed lifestyle, and identity obesity is not an exception which arises from mismanaging personal information leading to identity theft and fraud. For protecting our identities and living a balanced life, we must make our own assessment of which credit and other products are in our best interest, and, determine the maximum level of consumption beyond which we receive no additional benefit while we expose our health, credit worthiness and identity at risk. We must learn to notice when the cup is full and stop pouring, in all areas of our lives.

Part One:
Identity Theft Overview

Chapter 1: *Identity Theft*

In general, identity theft is referred to cases whereby someone's identity is used without authorization for gainful purposes. There are many criminal acts which can arise from identity theft cases including credit and medical fraud, unauthorized employment, and the sale of in-demand private information to media outlets. The consequences of identity fraud and disclosure of private information are sometimes devastating to consumers and may include ruined credit and inability to borrow money, false criminal accusations, commingled medical records, negative media attention, competitive disadvantage, wasted time, lost wages, warrants and jail time.

It is a well known fact that identity theft has been consistently on the rise and is an evolving crime. Although identity theft statistics are constantly revised and can be obtained from a variety of sources, the following statistics obtained from Javelin Strategy & Research seem to sum up most of the findings related to identity theft:

- In 2008, 10 million people were victims of identity theft (20% increase from 2007), and, in 2009, over 11 million people were affected by identity theft (10% increase from 2008),

- Fraud happens very quickly after an identity is stolen, usually within a week, indicating the importance of timely fraud detection to minimize the damage,

- Majority of victims detect identity theft 3 months after fraud occurs, and some discover fraud after 4 years or more,

- A victim may spend over 20 hours and $300 to resolve an identity theft case, and sometimes even months or years,

- Interestingly enough, stolen wallets and documents account for 43% of all identity theft cases indicating the low tech aspect of the crime,

- Identity fraud typically includes checking account fraud, unauthorized new credit accounts, credit card fraud and cell phone fraud,

- In more than 50% of all identity theft cases, the victim either personally knows the criminal or has done business with,

- Consumers are usually not liable for the fraud costs however, they still endure certain expenses related to their cases as well as some emotional and physical impact while dealing with identity theft,

- In 2009, over 220 million private customer records were compromised from businesses, and

- The estimated annual identity theft related costs for businesses is over $200 billions.

As we continue to face serious cases of identity theft, it is important to notice how the term "identity theft" has been broadly used to refer to many unrelated cases. The fact is that not all cases referred to as "identity theft" include the theft of exploitable personal information. If we separate the term into "identity" and "theft", we can conclude that not all "identity theft" cases involve exploitable information (identity) theft. For example, a misplaced document containing a list of birth dates should not be considered a case of identity theft because a) the list is not stolen and b) a date of birth means nothing by itself. However, once a list of birth dates which includes corresponding names or addresses is stolen, then the case can be referred to as a case of identity theft. Therefore, based on the broad definition and casual use of the term "identity theft", not all cases lead to fraud or other serious consequences.

Some identity theft cases may lead to identity fraud because specific and exploitable identity components are actually stolen for the purposes of committing fraud, however, identity theft may not result in identity fraud in all cases because of the casual use of the term "identity theft" in lost or misplaced cases of unexploitable information. Therefore, without "fraud" which is the intent and most likely the end result of actual identity theft cases, there is no harm in the act of "identity theft". Maybe disclosure of personal information such as medical records is worrisome if the information can be used against us, but a medical fraud is probably more deadly and concerning than the innocent disclosure of medical information because of the commingling of personal information which can occur during medical fraud. Let's further explore what I mean when I suggest placing our focus on identity fraud rather than the term "identity theft" which is casually used these days: 1) fraud is the main purpose of actual identity theft cases, 2) our identity is never totally lost or stolen, and 3) authorized sharing of our identity may result in fraud without identity theft. Let's analyze all three points and determine why the term identity theft may be misleading while identity crime or fraud should be the focus.

First, personal information is often stolen for fraud purposes. There are rare cases when personal information is stolen for non-fraudulent purposes such as curiosity or as part of another criminal act such as when a wallet is stolen for its cash. However, a stolen wallet does not make it a case of identity theft or the person an identity theft victim. What is the meaning of identity theft if no fraud can be committed? The term identity theft means nothing if no crime can be committed except maybe when our privacy is compromised. I may be worried about the disclosure of my private information because it can be used against me in some cases, but if criminals are not able to use my information against me such as not being able to illegally enter another country with my lost passport due to improved security controls at the airports or within the passport itself, then no crime can be committed and no harm is done. Therefore, the possibility and consideration of a crime is more important than the supposed case of identity theft. The casual use of the term "identity theft" in our society reduces the importance of the identity crime and it is often upon the discovery of a fraud that we realize our identity has been stolen.

Second, while criminals may use some of our identity components to commit various crimes, we are still capable of functioning within the society using our other identity components. For example, we may not be able to use the credit card that was stolen or apply for new credit cards due to the mess in our credit reports, but we can still use our other existing credit cards, go to the gym with our membership cards, and travel with our passports depending on which piece or component of our identity was stolen. You see, when we say our identity is stolen, it almost sounds like we no longer possess our entire identity and can't function at all.

Lastly, identity fraud can occur without identity theft. Many times, close relatives and friends with whom personal information is shared, abuse the trust and commit fraud with the entrusted information. Other times, some people may knowingly share their identity components with others to commit illegal acts or identity fraud. By doing so, they help their relatives or friends get medical help for example, without considering any serious consequences for themselves. Should these cases of identity fraud be considered the results of identity theft? Not really if personal information was shared willingly. There is no theft when information is shared willingly but we continue to broadly and casually define these cases as identity theft. This may surprise you but voluntary sharing of personal information with friends, family members, and coworkers is very common to help them get medical help, enter a building by using an access badge, get cash from the bank's cash machine, or even leave and enter countries illegally. Although, these acts are considered illegal and fraudulent, they are not the result of identity theft but rather the results of authorized sharing of personal information.

Chapter 2: *Fraud Schemes*

Fraud schemes typically include three major elements; fraud objective, required identity components, and execution plan. Sometimes the fraud objective might be cash or medical care which determines the required identity components such as insurance card, debit card and pass code to execute the scheme. Fraudsters will resort to various methods for executing the plan and achieving the final and desired fraud objective. Sometimes, a fraud scheme may require more than one identity component or piece of personal information in order to commit the specific fraud. For example, if a fraud objective is to steal cash from a bank Automated Teller Machine (ATM), a debit card and its access code or Personal Identification Number (PIN) are needed to execute the fraud scheme. As such, the fraud scheme should include steps to steal a debit card (or produce a counterfeit) along with its ATM access code in order to take cash out of the ATM. In the past, when debit cards could only be used to withdraw cash from the bank machines, the risks were lower than today since fraudsters can also go shopping with today's debit cards which also display the Visa or MasterCard logos and then sell the items in the open market to the highest bidder.

Here are a few methods that fraud schemes can be executed to steal identities:

Physical theft - in this scenario, personal information may be stolen from home, office, car, luggage, purse, wallet, briefcase, pockets, and others with whom personal information is shared. Such personal items or identity components may include credit cards, debit cards, passport, birth certificate, ATM code, driver's license, Social Security Number (SSN), account numbers, check books, and online account pass codes. The list of identity components which can be stolen to commit fraud is long and depending on the objectives of the fraud, only one or a few identity components may be needed to finalize the fraud schemes. According to recent identity theft statistics, theft of physical identity components accounts for about 50 percent of all identity theft cases. For example, stolen wallets consisting of one or more credit cards are often the root cause of credit fraud.

Spams – These are unwanted emails that we receive which are intended to accomplish certain goals. Spam emails might communicate certain information to the email recipient such as information about a product or service or include a link which will take the email recipient to a website or download a program on the user's computer when clicked. Such emails must be deleted immediately and removed from the trash folder. They must never be opened and the link within must never be clicked as it might install a dangerous software on the computer for the purposes of stealing personal information.

Pretexting – This term which is also synonymous with spoofing, impersonating, masquerading or mimicking is used to pretend to be someone else in order to extract desired information for committing fraud. An example of a pretexting is a spam phishing email which appears to be sent by a legitimate company. Once a consumer trusts the source of the email (because it appears to be from a company the customer does business with such as a bank), desired information may be shared willingly as requested by the email instructions.

Spoofing – As mentioned, spoofing is also another term used for pretexting to extract desired information from potential victims for the purposes of identity theft.

Phishing – Although, email communications may have various objectives, some are interested in specific information. In order to extract the desired information, some emails may appear to come from someone or a company the recipient recognizes. Generally speaking, these emails are well drafted and include a company logo to appear coming from a legitimate company. Sometimes, they are very hard to detect and really appear to come from a friend or a company we do business with. Sometimes, these spam emails are designed to take us to websites which either market a product or ask for our personal information. These are called phishing spams which are designed to extract confidential and personal information from people. Some of them are actually very well done and use fear tactics to lure people into sharing their information immediately and without any hesitation. For example, the phishing email might appear to be coming from a bank (pretexting) which states that "your account has been compromised and your cooperation is immediately needed". It further states the bank account has been frozen until the account holder provides additional information. It also states that all the scheduled payments and checks will be rejected pending the receipt of the additional information. This phishing email pretending to be coming from a bank is using scare tactics in order to entice the person to give away account passcode and other personal information immediately which can then be used to access and empty the account.

When someone receives such phishing schemes asking for personal information, it is recommended that the account holder logs into the account to verify if the account is really frozen and not accessible. If the account can not be accessed, the bank must be contacted directly by calling the number listed on the monthly bank statement and not the number provided in the spam email. And if the account can be accessed and the transaction amounts are verified as accurate, the email must be deleted and the account must be monitored for a few days to detect suspicious activities.

Social Engineering - This is another fraud scheme designed to extract information directly from people. Most often, someone approaches a potential victim by phone, email, letter or in person and pretends to be some authority figure that the victim recognizes such as a police officer, IRS agent, debt collector, or the security officer at the work place. These people again approach with a made up story and ask for certain information such as the Social Security Number or the account passcode. Such requests must be validated to ensure the individual and his requests are legitimate. To validate the legitimacy of such requests, an examination of a piece of identification and justifications for requested information must be completed. If the legitimacy of both the requestor and the request can not be fully and readily verified, the request must be rejected and no information must be shared. Also, identity thieves may approach unsuspecting consumers at the ATMs and other places to offer help such as with ATM code entry and system access while they steal the secret information and empty bank accounts.

Skimming – Card skimmers are devices which can read credit and debit card information in order to produce counterfeit cards. The skimming device can be placed on the ATMs where people insert their cards to withdraw cash, and as they scan their cards and enter the PIN, their card information is extracted and the entered PIN is either caught on an illegally installed camera or someone approaches the victim and uses the social engineering technique described above to offer help and extract the PIN from the victim. Also, the devices can be portable and used in public places such as restaurants. While the waiter carries the credit card away to charge the restaurant bill on the credit card, the device can be used to read all the card information in seconds which can then be used to produce counterfeit credit cards. Some restaurants in Europe and elsewhere require waiters to process the credit card transaction in front of the customer in order to defeat skimming. Consumers must be more aware and cautious of non-working ATMs and suspicious people, devices and places.

Shoulder Surfing - This is a casual fraud scheme used on unsuspecting people at the cash machines or on the computers. Fraudsters stand behind potential victims while they enter their codes into the cash machine or computer and observe the pass codes or other private information as they are entered or visible on the screen. When entering or reading confidential information in public places such as at the airport, coffee shops, banks or on the airplanes, we must notice how closely a person is standing behind us and cover our hand as we enter the pass code. To protect the privacy of the information we read on a computer, we can use a computer privacy filter which will prevent someone from reading the information displayed on the computer screen from a side angle.

Piggybacking - This illegal act is used to follow a person into a restricted area without having the required and approved access to the area. When an authorized person enters a secure area, the unauthorized person attempts to follow them while the door is open. In such situations, the person must be questioned regarding his business visit and accompanied to the final destination. If the answers are unsatisfactory, the incident must be immediately reported to an appropriate person for follow up.

Spyware (key loggers) - Illegal and unauthorized software may be installed on computers in order to spy on the activities of people using the computer and steal information. Such software can capture passcodes as they are keyed onto the keyboard (also known as key logger) or screen shots of confidential online pages such as account information pages. There are many anti-spyware programs that can be purchased and installed on computers to help prevent the installation of such software or detect previously installed software.

Chapter 3: *Identity Obesity*

I have concluded that identity obesity and underlying identity mismanagement by consumers and companies is the root cause of the identity theft epidemic. As I continue my research about the causes of identity theft and related risks or solutions, I am convinced that both consumers and companies unnecessarily accumulate, retain and share personal information at an alarming rate without the understanding of the risks and/or willingness to learn about and adjust their identity protection practices.

Let's first understand what I mean by identity obesity and why I think most consumers and some companies are identity obese. With regards to consumers, the best comparison can be made to our food consumption and weight obesity as I have previously discussed. *As eating more of the wrong things can lead to health and weight problems, managing too many personal information components in the wrong way can also lead to identity theft and fraud.* One of the reasons consumers excessively create, duplicate and share personal information is that they lack the basic understanding of the identity protection risks. For example, consumers continue to accumulate credit cards in which case the average consumer owns 8 credit cards or they carelessly create too many online accounts whether it's financial accounts or social networking accounts without the basic understanding of identity theft risks and related identity protection techniques. The big difference between weight obesity and identity obesity is that it's very difficult to reverse the damage caused by identity obesity. Once personal information is shared with other parties, it's extremely difficult if not impossible to recollect the shared information or stop the sharing cycle by parties we shared the information with in the first place.

Some companies also collect more personal information from their clients than they need in order to run their businesses. This careless practice leads to unnecessary information protection risks and costs. What makes it even worse is that companies which sell *exploitable* consumer goods and services such as credit cards fail to educate their customers about the identity fraud risks and best identity protection practices when using their products because customer education and awareness are not mandated by any laws and can also lead to lower sales. Companies in regulated industries such as healthcare, insurance and banking which are required to educate their employees about best information security and privacy practices are not required to educate their customers for protecting personal information outside of their business boundaries. Although educating customers is not required by current regulations, it is a good business practice and what some businesses fail to understand is that the long term cost of not educating their customers for preventing and detecting fraud is much higher than the cost for providing upfront and continuous awareness and education to prevent and detect fraud on a timely basis.

The long term consequences associated with unengaged customers include time and money spent for resolving increasing number of fraud cases, dealing with increased regulatory scrutiny, rebuilding corporate image, regaining lost customer loyalty and trust, and fighting multiple lawsuits.

As we discussed, identity obesity which is the excessive and unnecessary creation, retention and sharing of personal information can lead to a higher risk of identity theft and fraud if consumers mismanage their private and exploitable information. Let's first discuss what constitutes identity mismanagement in order to learn about the identity protection principles.

The Identity KAOS principles which I created and serve as the building blocks for developing the Identity Diet plan address the risks of identity obesity and identity mismanagement. Once you understand these principles, you will become aware of the identity protection risks and learn how to manage them. In summary, identity mismanagement can be summed up in 4 sections:

1. We might not know what exploitable personal information we possess and where they might be. For example, we might not know what information we have in our wallet or what identity component can lead to what type of crime.

2. We might not understand the risks of accumulating more personal information or using our personal information in an inappropriate manner. For example, we might write down our ATM code or keep applying for new loans on the Internet without any regard for the increased identity theft risks.

3. We might not properly organize our personal information and/ or monitor to detect identity theft. Most people don't have their identity organized for maximum recovery and protection let alone monitor to detect any unauthorized use.

4. And lastly, we might not secure and limit the sharing of our personal information. Most personal information components such as passports and credit cards must be physically secured and shared with caution if at all to reduce the identity theft risks.

We will further discuss the Identity KAOS principles in Chapter 11.

Chapter 4: *Identity Theft Spiral*

Identity theft and underlying crimes such as financial fraud, medical fraud, or illegal employment with someone else's name are on the rise. Identity fraud is nothing new and has existed for a very long time. These types of crimes further accelerated with the introduction of the Internet to the public and online dissemination of personal information in 1990s. As the online possibilities expand to help us connect to each other for business or social purposes, the risk of identity fraud and crime also increases.

The Internet has made it easy and faster for us to pay our bills, do business, meet people or share pictures and information, and therefore we are willing to trade our security for comfort. We tend to share too much information and blindly trust whoever is on the other side of the computer possibly thousands of miles away and in another country. This blinded trust is a source of rising identity fraud and criminal activities in our society.

The fact that we somehow know about the risks of online privacy but choose to ignore them is somewhat similar to the cash vs. credit card or casino chip principles. Have you noticed that spending actual cash is much harder than giving away casino chips or shopping with credit cards? I don't know why we tend to think twice as hard before giving away cash but somehow when we trade our cash for chips, credit cards or any other object, money loses its value and that's why casinos encourage their valued customers to trade cash for chips at every possible opportunity. The new slot machines even print receipts instead of dispensing cash for the credit balance. Similarly, we have traded our identity protection for comfort and networking on the Internet. Instead of driving to the banks to apply for credit cards, open bank accounts, and submit mortgage applications, or driving to the dealer to buy and finance a new car, or go to coffee shops to meet people, we search the Internet with such keywords as "cars", "loans", "relationships" and "credit cards" and instantly find thousands of networking sites, merchants, banks, car dealers and their easy applications. Without an identity theft worry in the world, we apply online to become members, buy cars, and obtain loans. The slow and ongoing change in the majority of business models from brick and mortar to online as well as our acceptance of the new way of life did not happen overnight. We went from restaurants to fast foods to drive-thru and now the Internet. I heard that we are even closer to a technology that will allow us to smell and taste things online and I believe it. We are moving fast toward a new territory with new or no rules. We don't exactly know where this new route will take us but it certainly introduces new identity theft risks that we need to consider. I like the Internet just as I like the fast foods and drive-thrus because they have made my life easy and I will not suggest going back to our old ways, however, we have to carefully manage the risks while we enjoy the comfort and speed of these services.

A balance between risks and reward is an old concept which must be considered to avoid online identity theft and spiral. As people rush to the Internet for comfort or to save time and meet new people, they expose themselves to huge identity theft risks and sometimes become victims of identity fraud as they carelessly share excessive amount of personal information. As they become identity theft victims, they go back to the Internet and search for companies which provide identity protection services. Without researching the companies or understanding the usefulness and the limitation of so many identity protection plans, they sign up for a plan within their budget and share even more personal information while buying these online identity protection services.

This is a trend that needs to be stopped if we want to protect our identities against fraud. One way to stop the trend is to be much more selective when using the Internet or sharing information with others. Being selective means using the Internet and sharing personal information only when absolutely necessary while making sure that we deal with the intended people, companies or websites. In fact, shouldn't we be selective with every thing else in life especially when we have selection options? Every action must have a reaction and over sharing of personal information will have negative consequences at some point.

Chapter 5: *Identity Theft is Unavoidable*

Although identity theft risks can be reduced to an acceptable and reasonable level if we take the time and effort to apply best identity protection practices in our lives, identity theft risks in general can never be completely and one hundred percent eliminated because consumers and businesses are interconnected and rely on each other to prevent identity theft. Also, in order to completely eliminate identity fraud, the opportunity, incentive and justification elements of fraud must also be eliminated. However, this is impossible because consumer identity obesity, business negligence and downward economy provide an ample opportunity and incentive for fraudsters to plan and execute their fraud schemes. As such, it would be unrealistically optimistic to expect and believe that identity theft is fully avoidable and one hundred percent preventable. However, we can reduce the occurrence and impact of identity theft through our actions and we can also prepare for the immediate identification and containment of fraud when it occurs.

Sometimes, consumer actions and inactions can lead to dire consequences but also the actions of other people and companies can also impact consumers. For example, if consumers accumulate endless number of credit cards, they increase their chances of facing identity theft (action taken) and if they don't regularly monitor their accounts and credit reports, they may face identity fraud (action not taken). On the other hand, consumers can do all the right things, and yet they have to deal with identity theft challenges because a company failed to properly secure its systems allowing hackers to remotely steal information or make unauthorized account changes in the systems.

Consumers collect all the credit cards and online accounts in the world and wonder how they became victims of identity theft or how they can avoid identity theft. On the other hand, they might take all the precautions to avoid identity theft like throwing away all the credit cards, shredding all personal documents, removing mails from mailboxes frequently and timely, reading all the corporate privacy policies and doing all the other right things, but yet they face identity fraud because someone posted their social security numbers on the Internet, or certain employee stored the personal information of customers on the laptop and took it home to be stolen from the driveway the same day. How do we control other people's actions that might affect us? As a society, we are so dependent on each other that either we all fail in the fight against identity theft or defeat identity theft with collective efforts. Companies develop and implement information security policies and privacy controls but all we need is a reckless, disgruntled or criminal employee to violate the corporate policies and create identity theft nightmare for millions of citizens.

In order to deal with identity theft, we must first accept that like most risks, identity theft is unavoidable and can occur for which we must and can prepare. Such preparations include continuous identity monitoring such as reviewing credit reports and bank statements for unauthorized transactions in order to detect identity fraud on a timely basis. Once fraud is detected, damage control steps and actions such as closing accounts, placing credit report freezes, and changing phone numbers must be taken to stop fraud expansion. The fraud detection, containment and recovery controls and actions will depend largely on the specifics of each fraud case.

Chapter 6: *Identity Life Cycle*

Identity life cycle must be understood when considering identity theft risks and best identity protection solutions. Below is a high level personal information life cycle also known as the Identity Life Cycle:

a. Information is born - a new piece of information is created by either you such as when applying for and obtaining a credit card or a passport, or by someone else such as a hospital issuing a birth certificate.

b. Information is maintained - after a piece of information is born or created, it is used, shared, and stored as it is maintained and managed through the identity life cycle.

c. Information is destroyed - at some point; personal information may be destroyed by either the identity owner such as when closing a credit card account and destroying the plastic or, by someone else such as a company closing the account and deleting the information, before or after a person's death. There is a risk that even a dead person's information can be misused after his/her death because the information was not properly destroyed upon his/her death. For example, misuse of dead people's social security card and number is very common because either death was not communicated timely to the Social Security Administration (SSA) or the administration failed to record death in their system on a timely basis, if at all.

As mentioned, any personal information can be created by a person or others. Such information is then maintained throughout its life cycle until it is destroyed. Take the example of a credit card. Consumers complete an application and provide personal information to a bank in order to obtain a credit card. They then maintain, use and share this credit card while the bank maintains the personal information initially provided to obtain the credit card. By applying for and obtaining a credit card, consumers place themselves in just two risky identity theft situations: First, the bank information may be stolen by identity thieves, and second, consumers may lose the credit card or its information may be stolen to produce counterfeit credit cards, resulting in credit card fraud.

A continuous self risk-assessment must be performed throughout the identity life cycle to determine:

a. Which information can lead to identity theft? In other words, which identity components are exploitable for fraud and other gainful purposes?

b. How can the information be exposed to identity theft risks? What are the threats facing the exploitable identity components?

c. What are the potential fraud implications? and,

d. What are the options for dealing with the identified risks? Consumers can mitigate the risks, decide to accept the risk or do nothing. For example, consumers may decide that the benefits of obtaining a credit card outweigh the credit card fraud risks when considering all factors such as building a credit history or spending borrowed money. Based on the risk assessment, a plan of actions can be developed to mitigate the risks which become part of the customized identity protection plan for each individual.

Chapter 7: *Fraud Drivers*

There are three main drivers or elements which allow individuals to commit fraud if all three elements are present. These elements are Opportunity, Incentive and Justification. Let's briefly explore them one at a time:

For fraud to occur, there must first be an opportunity for fraudsters in order to commit fraud. Depending on the type of fraud, the opportunities might exist abundantly. For example, a cashier might see the opportunity to take money from the cash register if there is no management supervision or watchful recording cameras. In the case of identity fraud, there are also many opportunities in many areas of identity fraud which we can spend countless hours and pages to discuss, however, consider the following example. A doctor might submit false insurance claims under a victim's name if the insurance company is not confirming the nature of the rendered services with the patient. The fact that the insurance company is not detecting false insurance claims presents an opportunity for the doctor to commit fraud without being apprehended.

Once an opportunity has been identified, the fraudsters should consider the incentive that a particular fraud might present. Taking the doctor example above, the incentive might be thousands of dollars in additional income per month for undelivered services. Depending on the individual's expectations, if a fraud incentive provides good value for the given risk and opportunity, then the thought of committing fraud moves one step closer to the execution of the idea.

And lastly, a good justification for committing the fraud closes the deal. In the same example, a good justification or rationalization on the part of the fraudster might be the fact that insurance companies are making too much money at the expense of the doctors and a few dollars out of their pockets are not going to hurt them.

As you can see, when it comes to protecting our identities against theft and fraud, we can manage the opportunity and incentive elements of fraud to some extent. For example, by properly protecting our personal information and identity components, we can reduce the opportunity element of fraud by not giving fraudsters a chance to take advantage of our information. And, by limiting credit limits, we can reduce the incentive element to the point where it does not make sense to take a risk and commit fraud.

As far as managing the justification element, there is not much consumers can do if fraudsters believe that no harm is done to consumers and only banks and businesses are affected by identity fraud. I think even fraudsters can benefit from some awareness to understand that their victims are not the only ones who suffer from their criminal acts, and, the harm will come back to hurt the fraudsters themselves either directly or indirectly because businesses will not hesitate to pass on the identity fraud costs to all their customers without any discrimination.

Chapter 8: *Identity Theft Laws*

Fair Credit Reporting Act (FCRA)

The Fair Credit Reporting Act (FCRA) is a Federal law which promotes the accuracy, fairness, and privacy of consumer information in the files of reporting agencies. Consumer agencies are not just limited to credit bureaus which sell information about consumer credit and payment histories. Other consumer agencies may sell information about check writing histories, medical records, and rental history.

Below is a summary of consumer rights under FCRA. You should understand these rights because the information that the consumer credit reporting agencies sell to companies to make business decisions belongs to consumers. Information being sold and used by third parties must be accurate, used fairly, and only be used by appropriate parties and with your express authorization in some cases. There is no doubt that some unethical companies or their employees may abuse consumer information by selling that information to just anyone without a valid reason, or without regard for its accuracy. There is also no doubt that companies which buy your information may make the wrong decisions based on potentially false information they were provided by consumer agencies and then treat your information without any regard for privacy. You need to learn and understand your rights to protect your information. Here's the list of your rights under FCRA:

1. *You must be told if information in your file has been used against you.* If anyone denies your application for credit, insurance or employment, or takes any other adverse action based on a credit or other consumer report, you must be told about the basis for their decision and given the name, address and phone number of the consumer agency that provided the information.

2. *You have the right to know what is in your file.* You can ask and obtain a free copy of your credit report if:

    *   Your application has been denied or adverse action is taken against you based on information in your file,

    *   You are a victim of identity theft and place a fraud alert in your file,

    *   Your file contains inaccurate information as a result of fraud,

    *   You are on public assistance, and

    *   You are unemployed but expect to apply for employment within 60 days.

3. *You have the right to ask for a credit score.* These scores provide information about your credit worthiness. Although you have to pay in order to obtain your credit scores from the credit agencies, in some mortgage transactions, you may ask for the mortgage lender for your score, or, the lender may send you the score used to deny your mortgage application.

4. *You have the right to dispute incomplete or inaccurate information.* If you notify the consumer agency about incomplete or inaccurate information in your file, they have to investigate unless your dispute is frivolous.

5. *Consumer reporting agencies must correct or delete inaccurate, incomplete, or unverifiable information.* Consumer agencies have 30 days to remove or correct inaccurate, incomplete or unverifiable information in your file. But, they may continue to

report the information to others if they conclude the information is accurate following verification.

6. *Consumer reporting agencies may not report outdated negative information.* Negative information should be removed from your file after 7 years. Bankruptcy information should be removed after 10 years.

7. *Access to your file must be limited.* Only parties with valid business needs can request to access your credit files. Such parties may include a creditor, insurer, landlord, and employer.

8. *You must give your consent for reports to be provided to employers.* Your written consent is required for employers to obtain your credit report.

9. *You may limit "prescreened" offers of credit and insurance products you receive.* You can stop the flow of prescreened offers by removing your name and address from the lists used to send prescreened offers. You can opt-out with nationwide credit bureaus at 1-888-5-OPTOUT or 1-888-567-8688.

10. *You may seek damages from violators.* You can sue in State and Federal courts for any violations of consumer rights under FACTA.

11. *Identity theft victims and active duty military personnel have additional rights.* Identity theft victims may request to place fraud alerts on their credit reports. Initial fraud alerts are good for 90 days and can be placed any time a person becomes an identity theft victim or even suspects he or she might become a victim. The initial fraud alerts can be renewed every 90 days but could also be extended to 7 years with a police report.

Active duty military personnel may also request to place active duty fraud alerts on their credit reports for 12 months which alert potential creditors to be more cautious with granting credit while they remain on active duty outside the country.

Please note that US States may enforce the Federal FCRA law, or have their own consumer reporting laws. In some cases, you may have more rights under State laws. Contact your local or State consumer protection agency or your State Attorney General for more information. For additional information regarding FCRA, you may visit www.ftc.gov or write to Consumer Response Center, Room 130-A, Federal Trade Commission, 600 Pennsylvania Ave. N.W., Washington, D.C. 20580.

Fair and Accurate Credit Transactions Act (FACTA)

The 2003 addition of FACTA (Fair and Accurate Credit Transactions Act) to The Fair Credit Reporting Act (FCRA) was intended to fight identity theft. While FCRA was originally created with the objective to promote the accuracy, fairness, and privacy of consumer information in the files of reporting agencies, the FACT Act was specifically intended to fight identity theft by giving consumers certain rights if they become or even suspect becoming an identity theft victim. Let's explore these rights:

1. *You have the right to ask that nationwide consumer reporting agencies place "fraud alerts" in your file.* Once you become an identity theft victim or even suspect you may be at risk of becoming a victim, FACTA gives you certain options to prevent or reduce the impact of identity theft in your life. Creditors typically grant new credit or increase existing credit based on the information in the consumers' credit reports. By placing a fraud alert, you notify creditors that someone other than you may be requesting for credit with your name, thus, putting them on notice to be more cautious when approving such requests.

2. *You have the right to free copies of the information in your file ("file disclosure").* A timely review of the credit reports will prove to be beneficial in ensuring the accuracy of the information in the credit reports and detecting identity theft. The discovery results of your review will determine the course of action that you need to take to resolve any issues. The frequency and timeliness of the review is extremely important in order to detect identity fraud. Depending on the type of alert that you may have placed on your credit report, you can access your credit reports once or twice a year. You can even get a free copy of your credit report every 12 months from all three credit reporting agencies even if you just suspect you may become a victim and without placing any fraud alerts.

3. *You have the right to obtain documents relating to fraudulent transactions or accounts opened using your personal information.* If

and when you come across a fraudulent transaction in your credit report, you can contact the creditors or the business owner of that transaction and ask in writing for documentation supporting the transaction. The business might ask you for certain document to validate your identity or ascertain an identity theft has occurred, however, even without a case of identity theft, you have certain rights with regards to inaccurate transactions under the FCRA.

4. *You have the right to obtain information from a debt collector.* Debt collectors just like the businesses they work for, must provide you with detail information about items that you believe are the result of identity theft. You can ask for the debt amount, creditor name and additional details.

5. *You have the right to ask that a consumer reporting agency block information from your file.* Under this consumer right, once you prove that you are a victim of identity theft by filing and submitting a police report, you can ask the credit reporting agencies to stop sharing the questionable information with others and a business or person may not sell, share or place the identified debt item for collection. Please feel free to remind both businesses and their debt collectors of the risk they may be running if they continue to harass you after a debt item is approved as an identity theft item and blocked by the credit reporting agencies. If you continue to be harassed by businesses and their agents (debt collectors), make sure you have your identity theft police report and the debt block request letter and approval with you when you consult a FACTA lawyer.

6. *You may prevent businesses from reporting information about you to consumer reporting agencies if you believe the information is the result of identity theft.* Just as you can ask the credit reporting agencies to block certain information from your credit report because they were the results of identity theft, under FACTA, you can also ask businesses to not report fraudulent transactions to the credit reporting agencies if you can prove you are an

identity theft victim by presenting a police report, and identify the questionable transactions. Afterwards, make sure you verify your credit report information to ensure businesses did not report the fraudulent transactions, and if they did, ask to remove them immediately.

Part Two:
Practical Identity Protection Solutions

Chapter 9: *Identity Theft Awareness*

The best approach for dealing with identity theft is prevention and an adequate awareness of the identity theft threats and appropriate solutions is the best approach for preventing identity theft and fraud. Unless identity theft risks are identified, best actions can not be taken and solutions can not be implemented to mitigate the risks. Individuals concerned with the security and privacy of personal information must increase their awareness of the identity theft risks by continually educating themselves about current threats, automated services, new laws and the best identity protection practices. Identity theft techniques are constantly evolving and new solutions and laws are introduced to counter these threats on an ongoing basis. Continued education is an absolute necessity to identify the identity theft risks and best possible solutions.

Consumer privacy is a new and evolving field which not only poses great risks if personal information is disclosed and misused but also very few people are aware of the risks or best identity protection practices. For example, social security numbers are available everywhere, at the doctor's office and on the Internet like pieces of worthless information; while the same social security numbers are heavily relied on to identify consumers. Businesses ask for social security numbers, names, phone numbers, addresses, and other pieces of personal information in public places and expect consumers to respond back with the information while surrounded by other people. We can not neglect the protection of our most valuable information and expect to see improvement in the battle against identity theft. As a society, we need to determine what information is critical to us, and apply more stringent security measures to protect them accordingly. For example, if we rely on social security numbers as a main source of identity validation, then we must treat them differently than our public information such as our home phone numbers.

In most cases, consumers are left in the dark with regards to the identity theft risks and best identity protection practices. Although businesses protect customer information within the boundaries of their business environment, they do not all educate their customers regarding the risks and best identity protection practices. Consumers in general don't know what information or identity components must be protected and also lack the necessary knowledge or "know how" to protect the information.

Consumers are constantly encouraged to obtain a bunch of credit cards or other credit products, forced to reveal their personal information in public, or enticed to apply for multiple mortgages or Home Equity Line of Credits (or HELOC) while they become more vulnerable to identity theft as they increase their exposure. Unfortunately, businesses do not provide risk awareness and identity protection education to their clients and fail to teach consumers that there is an increased and proportional identity theft risk with the number of times they share their information with others because they don't have any vested interest. Businesses might start to look at the issue and act differently when they realize that the long term fraud costs resulting from unaware and uneducated customers are more than the short term spending on consumer awareness and education for preventing and detecting identity theft fraud.

In conclusion, identity theft management starts with identity theft awareness. Consumers need to understand the identity theft risks, threats, consequences, target information, and learn how to protect their personal information. Businesses and consumers must work together to collectively protect personal information inside and outside the business boundaries. Consumers are generally the weakest link in the collective battle against identity theft and thus through education can help businesses reduce their fraud costs.

Chapter 10: *Identity Diet*™

Identity Diet™ is a program I have developed to help individuals create customized identity protection plans for their unique lifestyles. An Identity Diet plan is developed based on the Identity KAOS principles which we will discuss in the next chapter and the best identity protection practices listed in Chapter 12.

While individuals continue to become identity obese and mismanage their personal information, they lack an adequate level of awareness of the identity theft risks and knowledge of the best identity protection practices and solutions. Each identity is unique and presents a unique set of identity theft risks that should be handled carefully. Identity Diet™ was created to help consumers design a customized identity protection plan and:

a) Understand their unique identity theft risks;
b) Identify bad habits; and
c) Learn about and implement the best identity protection practices.

Most of us have either been victims of identity theft or know someone who has suffered from this crime. The fact is identity theft continues to grow affecting many people, and has even a greater impact on high value identities which provide bigger bang for the buck. High value identities such as high net worth individuals are among those on the list of high target identities. As such, the increased probability of identity theft occurrence along with the identity theft impact create a huge risk that should not be ignored and in fact should be promptly dealt with utilizing the latest fraud prevention and detection methods available. Consequences of identity theft if not prevented may include private information disclosure, identity fraud, criminal accusations, and negative media attention.

The Identity Diet™ plan can be designed and implemented by incorporating the eight Identity KAOS principles and applicable best identity protection practices. These identity protection principles along with the practical identity protection solutions in this book will allow you to create an actionable and customized identity protection plan for your life.

In order to develop the Identity Diet plan, you must take a hard look at how you manage your identity components. By learning about the Identity KAOS principles as well as the best identity protection practices, you will be able to develop a customized identity protection plan based on your understanding of your risks, ways to reduce your risks, and automated services available in the market such as credit report mentoring and change notification services. Many people sign up for identity protection services without the understanding of their usefulness and limitations. Most people think that by purchasing a credit monitoring service, all their identity theft problems will be solved. The truth is credit monitoring alone will not solve all your identity theft problems and is only a part of a comprehensive identity protection plan which still requires your involvement.

Please carefully read and understand the eight Identity KAOS principles in the next chapter followed by the best identity protection practices. These two sections should give you the necessary knowledge you need to create a customized Identity Diet plan for you and your family.

Chapter 11: *Identity KAOS Principles*

Identity KAOS™ is a set of eight identity protection principles, which if applied consistently along with the best identity protection actions discussed in the next chapter will reduce the risk of identity theft. This identity protection methodology must become part of your thought process and behavior when dealing with your personal information.

Personal and other valuable information is constantly created, stored, shared and destroyed. This is what I call identity life cycle. For example, right before you were born, information about you and your parents were collected by the hospital to issue your birth certificate upon your birth and physical characteristics. You must understand the identity life cycle, before you can manage and protect your personal information.

In some cases, you are in control of your information and therefore can protect your identity, and in other cases you are not. For example, you have no control over the birth certificate issued upon your birth as hospitals are required to report births, whereas when applying for a loan or using a debit card, you are somewhat in control as you can decide how many credit cards you want to own and how often or for what purchases you plan to use your credit or debit card.

Information in general is the most valuable commodity for everyone. Knowing what you don't know or not knowing what you know can be the difference between life and death. Information can destroy or save lives, break or build families, make people richer or poorer, provide competitive advantage and success for a company or bankrupt it, and destroy a personality.

Our focus here is to primarily address the identity theft crime which according to some statistics is on the rise. As more information is continuously created and shared in many forms and shapes, the security and privacy risks and their unwanted consequences are likely to increase for the foreseeable future.

Although every one is absolutely vulnerable to identity hijack including the dead, the identities of high credit worthy individuals, rich and famous celebrities, and corporate executives provide better fraud value and are more likely to be the targets of identity theft for two reasons: First, their identity may include better credit ratings and numerous valuable bank accounts and credit cards, and second, they are more visible and either loved or hated. For example, depending on the nature or reason of the information theft, stealing personal information of people with bad credit is not as useful as stealing the identity of a person with excellent credit and unlimited credit lines. Curiosity and espionage also can play a big role when targeting the high risk categories just mentioned. Again, a lot of people are identity theft targets, but some identities provide better value.

The Identity KAO principles along with the best identity protection practices presented in this book will provide simple ideas and solutions to help you:

a. Prevent someone from stealing your personal information as much as possible;

b. Detect signs of stolen information and any potential misuse of that information; and

c. Contain and minimize the damage inflicted as a result of the stolen information.

The Identity KAOS principles will guide your actions to minimize the identity protection risks which you can control. You will learn to think about identity theft threats as well as you conscious decisions for managing your information throughout its lifecycle.

The eight Identity KAO principles as they relate to personal information protection are summarized as:

- Knowing which identity component is exploitable for identity theft and fraud purposes,
- Knowing where the identified components are at all times,
- Assessing whether the identified components are needed,
- Assessing the way identity components are managed,
- Organizing identity components,
- Overseeing and monitoring the security of identity components,
- Securing identity components in accordance with organized categories, and
- Sharing personal information with caution.

The eight Identity KAOS principles are further discussed below in detail:

Know the Information

In order to start protecting your identity, you must first know 1) what exploitable personal information you possess and 2) where they are. These are the first and second Identity KAOS principles.

In every battle, you need to know your opponent (in this case, identity thieves), as well as their intentions and targets before defensive or protective measures can be put in place as part of your overall identity protection plan. In the case of identity theft, you must also identify your information (the target) and know exactly where they are at all times. As a starting point, an inventory of all your information assets such as credit cards, social security card, passport, birth and death certificates, and online accounts along with the related information such as issuer name, frequency of statements, address, phone number, account number, and date of issuance must be taken to create a complete list of all your identity components.

Then, locate where they are and include their location on the list. Knowing where your personal information is such as in your wallet, briefcase or office drawer along with the related information such as third party contact information can help you protect them accordingly and quickly report and recover from a case of identity theft.

Assess the Information

After you take an inventory of all your identity components and identify where they are, you need to asses whether 1) your personal information inventory list needs to be modified, and 2) your actions for using and managing your information is appropriate. These are the third and fourth Identity KAOS principles.

When assessing your personal information inventory items and actions toward them, ask yourself questions such as:

a. Do I need all these credit cards or online accounts? Think about whether you need all that is listed. Eliminate any you might not need and reduce your risk. Close the accounts properly by calling or writing to the credit card company, shred your cards, return the cards to the company if required, and mark closed with the date in your inventory list. With regards to online accounts, make sure you delete all personal information from your profile before you close the account.

b. Do I need to apply for another loan or open another account? Always ask yourself whether you need to add one more item to your personal information list. The less items on your list, the less you share your personal information with others, and less items you need to protect.

c. Which ones would I discard if I had to eliminate one or more? Eliminate the ones that provide the least benefit but provide greater or equal risks.

d. Do I have all the related information such as the company name, phone number, frequency of statements, password or the credit card number? Always include all related information in case you lose that piece of information. For example, writing and knowing your credit card number, the company phone number, or your passport number is very useful in case you and need to replace them immediately. Or, knowing the frequency of a certain statement will trigger an alert if you don't get the statement on time in which case you would have to follow up with the institution right away to make sure it was an honest mistake and not the result of an unauthorized address change.

e. Where is each individual piece of information kept? Ask yourself, where is my passport right now, or where is my xyz credit card? Is it in my wallet or in my briefcase? Knowing where it is will help you better protect your information.

f. Have I shared any of this information with anyone? Just think about how you use or share any of the information such as when, with whom, or how often. If you have sent any of the original pieces to anyone such as a birth certificate, make sure you follow-up and get it back. Sometimes, when you apply for a mortgage, some original documents are required from you, or a child's original birth certificate is required for certain transactions. Just make sure you get them back.

g. Do I use my information with caution? When carrying, sharing or using your information, always ask yourself questions like:

- Do I need to carry the original item?
- Must I carry multiple credit cards?
- Should I use credit or debit card for purchases?
- Should I change the location of my identity component?
- Do I really need to write down my pass code in plain English?
- Am I supposed to share my information?

In conclusion, assess your information and actions very carefully. This is a very important process that will change the way you think about and approach identity protection. This is not a one time process but a continuous one that requires your conscious involvement and awareness about identity theft as you manage your personal information on a daily basis. We will further discuss the best identity protection practices later.

Organize the Information

After you're done with creating a complete list of personal information and the location of your identity components, you need to properly organize and oversee your information. These are the fifth and sixth Identity KAOS principles.

In order to properly organize your information, you need to categorize the items in your inventory list based on their similarities and risk level. This is extremely important because the assigned risk level will determine the necessary and needed security measures which we will discuss in the next principles. Be very specific in your categorization, although you may consolidate a few categories when you organize your information.

For example, you may keep all home utility statements together or all credit card statements together. There are many benefits to categorizing your personal information items. First, you will find the information fairly quickly when needed. For example, we all know how daunting it can be to find and submit all required documents when applying for a mortgage. Second, we must categorize, because we must apply various levels of protection measures when dealing with our personal information. I personally keep my credit cards completely separate from my other documents for security reasons. This is a category I frequently visit to assess whether I need to make any changes. Some time ago, I came across a credit card that provided rewards for a child's higher education which interested me very much. More importantly, the credit card was offered by a bank I was already doing businesses with, so there was no additional risk of sharing my information with another bank. So, I jumped on the opportunity and called the credit card company to switch one of my existing cards from the same bank to this new card without completing another application. So, go ahead and organize your information, and don't forget to revisit the list once in a while and make adjustments as needed. Some of the categories may include:

a. Home utilities (water, power, gas, phone),
b. Credit cards,
c. Credit card statements,
d. Bank statements (checking, savings, mortgage),
e. Mortgage statements,
f. Brokerage statements,
g. Insurance policies (car, home, etc.),
h. Social security card or SSA annual retirement statements,
i. Passports,
j. Birth and death certificates,
k. Identity cards (ID, driver's license, green card, other),
l. School documents (school documents of all levels may include personal information),
m. W2 statements or any other work related documents, and
n. Tax return documents.

You also need to oversee or monitor your identity components to make sure they are not being used for identity theft purposes:

- Check your physical identity components periodically to make sure they are not missing and remain where they're supposed to be. Sometimes, our physical items such as credit cards can be stolen and the sooner we detect their absence, the sooner we can alert the banks and take actions to limit any potential fraud damages resulting from their theft.

- Monitor your monthly/periodic statements to verify their accuracy. Check your credit card transactions and make sure you have authorized them. If you do not receive a statement on time or notice incorrect items, follow up with the institution immediately and close your accounts if they have been targets of identity theft. Even if you think your statement balance should be zero because you did not have any transactions, it is still a very good idea to review the statements and verify no unauthorized charges are posted.

- Sign up with a credit monitoring service to receive alerts regarding any new accounts opened in your name or changes made to your credit reports. Most people know how to sign up for credit monitoring services but very few know how to follow up with the alerts they receive or overlook the importance of such activity. Check your alert notifications frequently and promptly follow up with each item and the credit monitoring company if you need help to clear all outstanding alerts.

Secure the Information

Once you're done with knowing, analyzing and organizing your information, you need to 1) secure and 2) share your information with caution. These are the seventh and eighth Identity KAOS principles.

Your personal information categories are now defined and we need to address the level of protection you want to assign to each category. Some categories may require the same level of protection measures such as bank and brokerage statements. I personally have a locked file cabinet where I keep all the statements related to credit cards, bank accounts, brokerage accounts, utilities, etc. I keep all the credit cards, passports, social security cards, and government issued documents in the ECD (Extremely Confidential Documents) category and under tight control. By the way, the personal information inventory list created in the first step falls under the ECD category as well because you have just listed extremely confidential information which needs to be protected. You may consider a fire proof safe box at home or an external safe box to keep all your valuable items including your personal information. You may even consider using both safe boxes to store most frequently used ECD items such as credit cards at home, and less frequently used ECD items such as social security cards, passports, and other government issued documents in the external safe box.

And finally, share you information with caution. Always question the need to share your personal information with others. Ask yourself and the requestor questions such as:

- Why is my information needed?

- How will my information be used?

- Whom will it be shared with and why?

- Where will it be stored and how will it be protected?

- What happens if I refuse to share my information?

- What law requires me to share my information?

- Is sharing my information increasing my identity theft risks?

One area where consumers are excessively sharing their personal information is related to credit and debit cards. We tend to use our credit cards for all transactions without giving much thought to the identity theft risks. Most often, there is no major benefit in using credit cards for small and frequent purchases such as when buying multiple daily coffees, however, the risk of identity theft further increases each time we share our credit card regardless of the transaction amount. Therefore it is very important to think about the risks of our actions before it's too late. Credit and debit card best practices are further discussed in the next section.

Chapter 12: *Best Identity Protection Practices*

We live in a world where identity theft is on the rise mainly because:

- It's easy to commit identity fraud due to increasing and available opportunities, justifications and incentives,

- As a society, we have been slow at addressing the issue especially in the areas of the identity theft laws, consumer awareness and education, as well as business responsibilities and efforts for protecting consumer information,

- The speed by which we collect, duplicate and share our personal information has accelerated at an alarming rate, and

- Consumers lack the basic understanding of the identity theft risks, their rights, business responsibilities, as well as knowledge about the identity protection services in the marketplace, their limitations, and how these services can automate and improve some of their identity protection efforts.

Below is a list of best identity protection practices that you can apply to your identity protection efforts.

Educate Yourself

Always attempt to understand the risks to your identity when managing your information. Make sure you educate yourself about the latest threats, market solutions and the laws in order to understand your rights and business obligations when it comes to your privacy. Knowledge is power and sometimes, it also gives you free stuff. For example, the latest laws allow consumers to get free copies of their credit reports every 12 months from all three credit bureaus, and although, most companies brag about giving consumers free copies of their credit reports, while selling them other services, you can get your free credit reports yourself from www.annualcreditreport.com. So, educate yourself to better protect your identity and save money along the way. Also visit www.identity-theft-awareness.com for free articles and sign up for the monthly newsletter to get the latest information as they become available.

Select Service Providers Carefully

Many of us use the services of professionals such as home or office cleaners, tax preparers, lawyers and others. You need to carefully assess whom you share your valuable information with and how they protect them. You also should carefully assess who must access your home or office where you might store personal information. Get references, interview them, visit their offices and observe how organized and secure their environment is, and always monitor them while they are on your home or office premises.

Audit Your Service Providers

In some cases, you may want to request and complete a background check to ensure the service providers you have engaged or plan to hire have clean backgrounds free of any past criminal activities, especially before letting them into your homes and offices for cleaning or babysitting purposes. However, you need to first make sure they are who they say they are before you perform a background check. A clean background means nothing if the background does not belong to the service provider. Therefore, make sure you ask for as many pieces of identification as possible to reasonably confirm their identities before a background check is completed.

Share Information with Caution

Consumers are constantly forced to share information with others whether it's at the doctor's office, or following a car accident. Make sure you analyze the reasonableness of the requests and only share the minimum information when needed. For example, limited information must be exchanged during a car accident such as name, license plate number, driver license number, phone number, and insurance information. Avoid sharing more information than necessary for the particular situation. Excessive sharing of your personal information further increases your risk of identity theft. Of course sharing personal information with trusted family members may present a lower identity theft risk than sharing information with a stranger; however, trusted family members may unknowingly place your identity at risk by mismanaging your shared information.

Be Aware of Your Surrounding

Always assess the environment where you share information or complete a transaction. For example, notice who is standing behind you at the bank's Automated Teller Machine (ATM) and how close they are to you, or who can hear you when you share your information with a doctor, friends and colleagues. Also, when using your wallet in public, make sure items containing your personal information such as a driver's license are not visible and kept confidential. Some wallets are designed to hold pictures or a driver's license without having to take them out before they can be presented to others; however, they also present a risk from an identity theft standpoint when they unintentionally become visible to strangers while taking out cash or credit cards.

Cover PIN Entry with Your Hand

One of the ways identity thieves empty checking accounts is by using ATM skimming and Personal Identification Number (PIN) extraction schemes. In the identity theft overview section, we discussed what ATM skimming means which is a device placed on ATMs to copy the card information and create a counterfeit debit card. Also, while you enter your PIN to withdraw cash, illegally placed cameras or social engineering techniques are used to obtain your PIN which allow thieves to withdraw cash from your accounts very quickly. Although, it's very hard for consumers to detect installed ATM skimming devices, they must make every effort to safeguard their PINs as without the PIN, thieves will not be able to easily take cash out of the bank account. Cover your finger movement as you enter your PIN and do not share your code with any approaching person. If you are unable to access the system after you enter your PIN, this might be a potential scheme to force you to enter your PIN multiple times or approach you to offer help.

Know the Latest Consumer Rights

You should be aware of your rights and business obligations to better protect your identity. For example, make sure you know the difference between a fraud alert and a credit freeze before signing up for various services. Or, know your consumer rights and business obligations under FACTA and FCRA. These laws force companies to protect consumer information and require companies to obtain consumer authorization for sharing their information with non-affiliated parties. In addition, companies must in due time, notify consumers of any security breach incident that might expose the consumer identity to fraud and disclosure. Stay on top of your rights and when your personal information is exposed to identity theft risks due to someone else's negligence, ask the negligent party for identity theft protection services and in some cases, consider consulting a lawyer.

Know the Corporate Privacy Policies

Companies must now share their privacy policies with their consumers to express what they intend to do with the consumer's personal information. Companies must in particular notify their customers whom they intend to share the customer information with and allow consumers to opt-in or opt-out of such information sharing plans with non-affiliated business partners. Although somewhat of a daunting task, it's a good idea to be familiar with privacy policies of companies with whom you share your information.

Place Fraud Alerts on Your Credit Reports

You can place fraud alerts on your credit reports by contacting one of the credit reporting agencies. Placing a fraud alert can help stop an identity fraud before it happens as your identity should be validated before credit is granted, although, credit grantors are not obligated to contact and validate your identity. In other words, you may place a fraud alert on your credit report, but still be a victim of credit fraud because a business failed to validate the identity of the requestor. An initial fraud alert is good for 90 days and can be renewed every 90 days. There are automated services which can accommodate the placement of the fraud alerts on all your credit reports every 90 days. If you are a victim of identity theft and have a police report, you can also place an extended fraud alert which is good for 7 years. As I mentioned, you don't need a third party to place fraud alerts on your credit reports, but it's a good idea to automate the placement of initial fraud alerts since you may forget or procrastinate when it's time to renew the fraud alert again.

Use Cash Whenever Possible

When you use cash instead of a debit or credit card for purchases, you limit the sharing of your card information with others. When you share your card information with others, you rely on the external party to protect your information and thus lose control of your personal information assets. Plus, your card information might be exposed every time you use it. Always plan your purchases in advance and have enough cash for routine and small purchases. Use your credit card selectively and for big items to take advantage of rewards or warranty options. Small item purchases do not provide enough value for the risks they present when using a credit card. Using gift cards to purchase small and frequent items like coffee is a great way to prevent identity theft.

Use Store Gift Cards

Using store cards or gift cards is a great way to prevent identity theft and limit your losses. First, you can load your gift card with cash when its credit balance becomes low. By using cash instead of credit card for re-loading the store card, you avoid sharing your credit card. Second, by using the store card for frequent and small amount purchases, you limit the excessive use of your credit or debit cards which might place your checking account or credit card at an increased fraud risk. However, if you lose your store card, the most you can lose is your cash balance on the card without compromising the protection of your identity.

Assess Credit Card Offers

Think before you accept a credit card offer. By blindly accepting all credit card offers, not only you do not carefully asses your credit needs and the best credit card to satisfy your needs whether it's low rates, high reward points and credit limits, but you also increase your risk of identity theft and credit card fraud by owning one additional card and sharing your personal information. Many people are identity obese in this area where the average person owns 8 credit cards. This area is of very high concern from an identity fraud standpoint because not only credit cards present great opportunities for credit fraud, but also the consumer carelessness in this area provides the opportunity the fraudsters need to easily commit fraud and steal cash or buy things. Therefore, you should have fewer cards and select the best credit card that's right for you. I suggest owning 2 credit cards with the right credit limits for our needs and lifestyle. One of them can be used for daily usage and the second one can be kept in a secured location to be used as backup when our first card can no longer be used because it expired, is being replaced due to loss or theft, or any other plastic problems.

Have a Credit Card Inventory

Not only you should know how many credit cards you have but you must also know their locations and details such as card number, issuing bank and the contact number in case you lose them. In the Identity KAOS principles, we discussed creating an inventory of all personal information for assessment, organized protection and quick recovery purposes. The credit cards must also be listed in the identity inventory list for the purposes listed above. Another way to keep track of the credit card details is to securely store a statement for each credit card just in case such information is quickly needed. You replace the older statement as you receive new ones if you don't want to keep all of them. The credit card statements and the identity inventory list must be secured at all times for obvious reasons.

Limit the Number of Credit Cards You Own

As mentioned, the best number of credit cards to own is two for most people. The first one can be used for daily purchases and the second for backup in case the first one is lost, stolen, cancelled or does not work. Some credit cards offer better value than others while all credit cards present a set of credit fraud risks. Keep the ones that provide the best value to match your credit needs and lifestyle such as low interest rates, purchase warranty, travel insurance, cash rebates, and mileage points.

Note: A high credit limit card that you rarely or never use further increases your risks. Select a credit limit for your unique purchasing needs and not more. This is different for everyone as our needs are different. Only you can decide what credit limit is best for you given your credit needs and tolerance for credit fraud risk. For example, a person whose credit limit on one of the cards is $500 has a lower fraud risk than a person whose credit limit on a similar card is $5000 if and when the card is compromised and used to commit fraud.

Use Your Cards with Caution

You should use a credit card in such a manner that reduces your identity theft risks and increases the value the credit card provides. For example, you should use credit cards for big item purchases to obtain extended purchase warranty for damaged or stolen merchandise, cash rebates, mileage points, etc. Frequent and small purchases such as daily parking or transportation tickets do not provide a huge value for credit card users and increase your identity theft risks by frequently sharing your information with various people. Use cash or gift cards instead for small and frequent purchases.

Know Where Your Credit Cards Are

If you must have more than 2 credit cards, you should know where they are at all times for a quick assessment and recovery in case of loss or theft. You should know which one (s) is in your wallet or purse and which ones are securely stored away. This way, if you lose your wallet, you don't have to guess which cards were lost in order to quickly notify the banks and request replacement.

Don't Carry All Your Credit Cards

Reduce the number of credit cards you carry with you. Limiting the number of credit cards you carry in your wallet can reduce the risk of credit card fraud if your wallet is lost or stolen. In fact, you should assess and reduce other contents of your wallets and carry less identity components to reduce your risks. As mentioned before, theft of physical items such as wallets, checkbooks and documents account for fifty percent of all identity fraud cases.

Notify Loss, Theft or Fraud Immediately

You should notify the banks immediately when you become aware that your credit card is stolen, lost or was targeted for fraud. Timely notification can help prevent fraud and potentially relieves you of any responsibility for fraudulent charges. Therefore, when you lose a credit card and could not find it, don't search for ever because late notification can inflict financial losses and point the responsibility to you. Search for a reasonable period of time and then notify the credit card company if you don't find it, especially if you don't know when or where the card was last used. Most people are so attached to their personal belongings that they would look for them for a long time. This is not very wise when it comes to misplaced credit cards and other identity components such as passports. It's very easy to request a card cancellation which has no consequence on your credit rating. In fact, it would be prudent to cancel lost cards and prevent potential fraud.

Occasionally, we might also forget to retrieve our debit card from the ATM at the conclusion of out transaction. Although, the cards left behind are swallowed by the machine within seconds, you never know for sure, therefore, it is also a good practice to notify the branch or the customer service and report the incident. Most often, the debit card is cancelled and a new one is sent to the home address on file.

Use Credit before You Use Debit

We all get asked if we want to use our card as a debit or credit at the stores. In fact, sometimes the stores even force us to use our ATM cards as debit cards by asking for the Personal Identification Number (PIN) or card code when we slide the card. The reason is that businesses lose money when we use our cards as credit instead of debit because they have to pay commissions to Visa, MasterCard and others. When you use your debit card, you must enter your PIN to authorize the transaction and the money is taken out of your checking account to pay for the purchase and involves no cost to the merchant. However, by using your PIN, you reveal another personal secret that if compromised, can be used for cash withdrawals from your account. When fraud occurs using your PIN or password, it's very hard to prove innocence and you may be liable for the entire fraud charges. However, with a credit card, you liability is limited to $50 when you discover fraud and report the incident within 60 days. Think again before you use your ATM card as a debit card next time.

Don't Keep Your PIN with Your Credit Cards

Most credit cards provide a PIN or code for cash advances. You can use the PIN to get cash from any ATM up to the allowed amount from your credit card. Therefore, losing your credit cards along with the PIN is a wonderful opportunity for fraudsters. Keep the PINs separately in a secured location until needed. Never write them down and place them next to your credit cards.

Keep Your PIN Safe

You should select a PIN that is unique enough that no one can guess or knows. You should also never share with others or write your PIN down. If you must write your code down because you deal with millions of passwords these days, make sure you secure the code by writing it in a unique way that only you can understand or by encrypting the file when the code is digitally stored. Another suggestion is to never keep the PIN or code with its associated account. For example, if you lose your online bank account ID along with its associated pass code, your account can be accessed and face unauthorized transactions.

Shred Cancelled Cards

From time to time, you may decide to cancel a credit card because you found a better one that meets your needs. Or, you might get a new card to replace the expired card. In such cases and after you activate the new card, you must properly shred the card where your name or card number appear as well as where the magnetic strip is located.

If you no longer need a credit card, you must cancel the card by calling the bank and then shred the cancelled card. Any delay in cancelling or shredding the cards may result in additional risks of disclosing the card information which can be used for fraud purposes.

Report and Replace Missing Cards

You might notice some of your existing credit cards are missing for whatever reason or you might notice new cards have not arrived to replace your expired cards. In such cases, you must report the situation to the issuing banks immediately to avoid potential fraud. In most cases, the banks will close the missing cards and send you new ones. If your existing cards are missing, don't look for them forever which might provide a window of opportunity to fraudsters. The key is to reports incidents and even suspicious activities promptly to minimize exposure and damage.

Limit Storage of Personal Information on Your Computer

Depending on many factors, you should attempt to limit storage of confidential information on your computers. Important factors for deciding whether or not to store confidential information on computers include: 1) you often carry your computer to public places, 2) your documents or computer are not encrypted, 3) your computer lacks minimum security software, and 4) you use the computer to connect to the Internet.

Use Security Software

When using a computer to access the Internet, you should use all required software to protect your computer and children. Use software to control spam, viruses and spyware, and protect emails, applications, instant messages, and Internet traffic with a firewall. You should consider using software to block unwanted sites when children use the same computer to access online games or websites.

Remove Resumes from Online Sites

Many people post their resumes online to find jobs. You must keep track of online locations where you post your resumes and remove them promptly when you find a job. Hopefully, the posted resumes do not include much personal information other than name, home address, email address and phone number. Even then, I think it's better to remove them completely when there is no need to share the smallest piece of personal information with the world.

Separate Internet and Admin Computers

We use computers for various reasons but mainly for Internet access and other things such as word processing. Connecting a computer which has a lot of stored confidential information to the public domain or the Internet is not recommended. By not connecting a computer with confidential information to the Internet, the confidential information can not be stolen when the system is accessed by unauthorized hackers. Some of us have more than one computer at home or office and we tend to use them all for all purposes. I suggest using a dummy computer with no personal information or documents for Internet access while using another computer for document editing, storage and other purposes.

Lock Computer Screen When Away

Locking a computer screen at home where children might play with the computer or at a public area such as a coffee shop or airport when you step away for just a few minutes is a good idea to protect your information displayed on the computer screen. Privacy filters are also very useful to blind nearby predatory eyes while working next to a stranger on a plane or elsewhere.

Use Privacy Filter

A privacy filter covers the screen of your computer so that a side view is eliminated.

Whether you work on confidential information in public places or your share your office with other colleagues, it's very important to use a laptop privacy filter such as the 3M privacy filter to block the screen view from anyone viewing the computer from a side view. Screen privacy filters have additional benefits such as glare reduction and computer screen protection against scratches and fingerprints.

Although, a privacy filter can protect against side view, you should make sure no one is behind you when accessing confidential information on your computer in public places.

Leave Your Laptop at Home

There are many instances when we have to carry our computers with us such as during a business trip. However, there are also times when we carry our computers loaded with confidential information to places where we don't really need or even use our computer. For example, when we travel for pleasure, we might need Internet access to check emails but most likely, there are computers at the hotels where we stay that we can use for a few minutes to check emails. Before taking your loaded laptop with you, think about the consequences. If you must have a computer with you, make sure it has no stored personal information.

Encrypt Your Information

If you have to store personal information on your computers, especially the ones that you carry with you to places, you must think of the worst case scenarios and protect your information by encrypting your laptop. This way, even if your laptop is stolen or lost, you can rest assured that the encrypted information is useless to others without the password.

Be Careful with Online Accounts

There are many security risks associated with online accounts. Some of our accounts might be used for banking or social networking purposes where personal information is stored and shared. Be selective when creating new online accounts, choose strong passwords, and always sign out of the accounts especially when using public computers. Most of us have more accounts that we can handle or remember to access a second time. Therefore, it's very important to be selective. Frankly, many of us have opened so many online accounts that we don't even remember that they exist let alone remember the login credentials to access the accounts. Some of the accounts may not be as harmful as others, but depending on what the site is used for or the personal information we entered when we initially created the account, the risks might be really high if we don't properly take care of them. So, I suggest finding a way to identify all of the online accounts as required by the Identity KAOS principles. Then, decide which ones you need to maintain, and which ones you can eliminate. As you go through this process, be very selective and attempt to own as few accounts as possible. Once, you identify and assess your accounts, consolidate duplicate accounts if possible and close the unwanted ones. For example, you may consolidate some financial accounts such as multiple IRA or savings accounts, or, you might decide to forego one social networking site for another. Once you clean up your online accounts, think hard before you open another account going forward.

Don't Trust Every Identity

There is a difference between meeting people online and in a bar or coffee shop. At a bar, you can physically inspect a person such as their behavior, their identity cards and other physical patterns. However, it's a different story online. An old person can be young, a male could be a female, or a Jane could be a John. It's very hard to know who is who. Even a nice picture online may not be the real person. Therefore blindly trusting an online identity without validation can help facilitate identity theft especially if such interactions involve sharing personal information. That being said and knowing how addicted we are to the online world, be polite by trusting first but always verify and validate the person before your share any personal information, exchange something, or agree to meet the person alone.

Delete Unrecognized or Suspicious Emails

When you receive emails that you don't recognize, look suspicious and appear to be spams, don't open any document attached to the email and delete the email immediately. Opening documents which may contain malicious programs can harm your computer and install spyware to monitor your behavior or steal your information while you enter them such as passwords you enter to access your online banking accounts.

Erase All Computer Data before Discard or Give Away

So often, people sell or give away their computers to charity without erasing and backing up important information from their computers. You never know where your donated computer ends up in the world so it's very important to erase all information. There are places which will clean up your computer hard drives before you give them away.

Use Trusted Computers

When accessing the Internet especially when using online banking to pay bills, always attempt to use trusted computers such as your office or home computer. When using public computers for highly sensitive transactions, consider the trust level you have with the facility providing Internet access. There are public computers that are more trustworthy than others and as such may not have spyware and predatory eyes to spy on your entered passwords to gain unauthorized access to your accounts and other sensitive information. For example, a library computer or a professional association computer is less likely to have malicious software or installed predatory cameras than an Internet café you just discovered while traveling.

Ignore Prank Internet Messages

Once in a while, we may get Internet messages from a site to which we belong. Such messages may come from people we don't recognize although they might claim or appear to know us. Ignore such messages if you don't recognize the sender. Remember, the sender might appear to be your sister, friend or someone you know. They're not always who they say they are. Validate their identity by asking a few personal questions before any further communication.

Separate Computer Accounts

If multiple users use the same computer, it's important to separate the administrative account from all other user and guest accounts. The two main reasons for this practice are that first, the administrative account password is needed every time a program attempts to install software or update existing software, and second, personal files stored on the computer can not be accessed or accidentally deleted, modified or sent over the Internet by other users on the same computer such as small children.

Lock Doors and Cabinets

You may file important documents at your home or office cabinets and drawers. Make sure you lock them up and keep the keys well secured. For recovery purposes, I keep two sets of keys in separate places just in case one is lost.

Choose a Fireproof and Waterproof Box

Store your important documents in a fireproof and waterproof box to limit damage and loss caused by fires or flooding. Such documents may include your passport, house title, and other government documents.

Use a Safe Box

Using a heavy safe box is not only a good idea to store jewelry, but it can also be useful in securing important documents such as passports. During casual burglaries, heavy safe boxes are less likely to be broken into or taken out of the house.

Keep an Eye on Your Mailbox

Many of today's mailboxes are not secured, especially the home mailboxes which are located on the street and accessible by the public. Either lock the mailboxes or collect your mails as soon as they're delivered. The longer your mails remain unsecured, the more vulnerable they are to theft and disclosure.

Keep an Eye on Your Visitors

When you let strangers into your house for personal services, always closely monitor their movements. Stay with them during their entire stay. An opportunity is one of the fraud elements and therefore an unsupervised home with a lot of cash, jewelry and other valuables may just provide the opportunity that a visitor needs to become a fraudster.

Secure Your Car Items

Sometimes, we have to drive to places with our personal documents to apply for passports or copy documents. You should make sure you never leave the documents for long periods of time in the car, especially when parked all night in quiet and dark streets. Make sure you complete the tasks at hand as soon as possible and file your documents in their secure locations upon return.

Get Acquainted with Your Wallet and Purse

We all have many important items in our wallets and purses and sometimes we may not have a complete list of the items. As such, when we lose our wallets, we may not immediately know what items were lost in order to quickly take the appropriate actions. In addition to known items like a driver's license, most of us carry more items that we can readily identify in our wallets. Occasionally, take an inventory and update your inventory list for quick recovery. As previously discussed, stolen and lost wallets or other physical items and objects containing personal information account for half the identity theft cases. By just taking some precautionary measures to limit your exposure to identity theft such as eliminating the unnecessary items you own and carry around or knowing what items are in your possessions and securing them at all times, you can reduce your identity theft risks by about 50 percent.

Avoid Loud Discussions in Public

Whether we are sharing information at the doctor's office or having a casual conversation with a friend or colleague, we should avoid loud discussions and keep the conversation down to avoid accidental sharing of confidential information with others.

Don't Leave Personal Items in Hotel Rooms

Unless there is a safe box in the hotel room, you should always carry your important items with you such as your passport when traveling abroad. Leaving your items unsecured in the hotel room means you fully trust the cleaners and others who have the keys to your room. Be in control of your items at all times.

Carry Only the Minimum

You should attempt to carry only the minimum and necessary items when you travel. For example, you need a passport to enter another country but you don't always need your marriage certificate, birth certificate or multiple credit cards for your visit. Assess your situation and carry only what you need.

Take Copies When Possible

When you have to carry and present certain documents, inquire about whether you can present a copy of the document. This way if you lose the document, you only lose a copy and not the original.

Have Visual Control of Your Items

Whether you're going through the airport security checks or storing your items on the overhead compartment of an airplane, make sure you have perfect visual to detect theft.

Maintain Security at the Gym

When going to the gym, always carry the minimum and lock your items. Choose a locker that is located in a high traffic or high visibility area of the locker room.

Refinance with Care

Many people refinance more frequently than they should thus unnecessarily and excessively sharing personal information with others. Think about your refinancing objectives, do your homework and when a good deal comes along, jump on the opportunity. With careful planning, you can reduce your refinancing costs and identity theft risks by limiting the number of times you refinance.

Don't Use a Web Application to Prepare Taxes

When we use a web application vs. software installed on our own computer to prepare our taxes, we store our personal information on a third party server which is not a very good idea as we don't know how secure their computer systems are. However, when we purchase and install tax software such as Turbo Tax on our computers to prepare our taxes, we store our tax information on our own computers. That being said, make sure your computer is erased of all tax information before you dispose of it.

Select Well Known Tax Software

When purchasing tax software, always buy well established software such as Turbo Tax to ensure there are no major bugs, and have good functionality and security. Many times when new software is introduced, there are multitudes of problems that need to be detected, reported and fixed. However, older software is usually gone through many fixes and functionality reviews to provide the best service in the most secure manner.

Freeze Inactive Accounts

You may have some accounts that you need to keep open but are hardly ever used; in such cases you can freeze the accounts to stop any use of the accounts until the accounts are activated for use again. A good example is our cell phone account. When we travel internationally for an extended period of time and leave our cell phones behind, we can deactivate the phone service until we are back and need our phones again. This concept can be applied to many other unused accounts.

Limit Cash Balances in Your Checking Accounts

Checking accounts are used more often than savings accounts and other cash based accounts. As such, the account information is shared often and more vulnerable to unauthorized use. Unauthorized cash withdrawals are often not protected from liability similar to credit cards where consumer losses are limited to $50. By limiting cash balances in checking accounts, you limit your losses in case of checking account fraud which is one of the top fraud categories. You may limit your checking account balance in accordance with your needs and risk tolerance while you keep the rest in a saving account.

Consolidate Your Accounts

If you have multiple IRAs and 401Ks, you should consider consolidating them into fewer accounts for better control, less risk and effective monitoring. Most people have many checking and other financial accounts, especially, when they go from one company to another and participate in their 401K programs. We often leave the accounts open for no reason and never consolidate as we change employments. I suspect that people who change jobs frequently while they participate in retirement programs without consolidating their accounts, probably don't even monitor their accounts to detect errors and fraud. Reviewing these accounts frequently can provide us the opportunity to detect potential fraud or errors on a timely basis.

Distribute Money across Multiple Savings Accounts

Although limiting checking account balances and consolidating financial accounts such as IRAs are good ideas for effective monitoring, detecting fraud and limiting fraud losses, placing lifetime cash savings into a single savings account is not a very good idea because most savings accounts are only insured by the government up to a certain amount, and in case of account fraud, lifetime savings can perish at once. When attempting to decide which accounts to consolidate and which ones to keep separate, the question of *risk, benefit and effort* must be considered. For example, in the case of savings accounts, having multiple accounts limits financial losses up to certain amount if the bank fails, and lowers risk of fraud if one account is compromised, however, requires increased effort for monitoring multiple accounts. Therefore, if you can tolerate fraud losses up to your account balance, then you're fine; otherwise, you need to rethink the distribution of your lifetime savings across multiple accounts to reduce your risk.

Select Strong Passwords

When deciding what passwords to select, always remember to select passwords that you can remember without being forced to write them down, and which are not simple enough for others to easily guess. Some people may select their first name for their password which can easily be guessed. To ensure your passwords are easy to remember but hard to guess by strangers, always select passwords that are at least 6 characters long, include letters and numbers (alphanumeric) as well as capital letter and/or special character. The passwords can be an abbreviated version of a phrase related to the account. For example, for a travel site account, I may choose the password "IloveSD2" for "I love San Diego too".

Never Write Down Your Passwords

You should avoid writing your passwords down to prevent their loss and disclosure. However, if you have to absolutely write them down because there is no way you can memorize hundreds of passwords, make sure a) the associated account ID is not listed next to the password, b) passwords are written in a code language that only you can understand, and/or c) the list is encrypted or well protected in a secure location. It's also a good idea to select and use different pass codes for various accounts because if one pass code is stolen, it can not be used to access all other accounts.

Change Your Passwords Periodically

Changing passwords every 90 days or so is a very good idea to stop unauthorized access. For example, if someone has stolen or guessed your password to access your bank account or read your emails, changing your old password to a new password, will put an end to their unethical practice. When considering the frequency of password change, you must remember that changing passwords too often can cause you to not remember your passwords and changing them less often can let fraud continue for a lengthy period of time.

Never Share Your Passwords

You should never share your passwords with anyone unless you absolutely have to in which case you should change the password again after the other person is done with your password. This practice doesn't mean you don't trust your loved ones but it reduces the accidental loss or theft. So, if you have to absolutely share a password with a loved one for a one time event, make sure you change the password thereafter to prevent theft and blaming each other. This rule also applies to work related passwords shared at the office. This will make sure you are not held responsible for the actions of others.

Keep a List of Your Identity Components

When you keep a list of your identity components and related information, you can periodically assess and decide which ones you no longer need or pose an unnecessary identity theft risk. The list can also help you quickly identify which item is missing from your control and report the incident to the appropriate parties for recovery and damage control purposes. Some items that can be listed include passports, credit cards, IDs, and other official documents. Please refer to the Identity KAOS principles for additional information regarding this practice.

Categorize, File and Secure

Identity components must be categorized and filed carefully for a quick recovery and security purposes. For example, tax documents, bank statements, credit card statements, insurance documents and other items must be organized and stored in accordance with their nature and sensitivity. Items of sensitive nature such as passports and unused credit cards must be kept securely in a locked environment. Please refer to the Identity KAOS principles for additional information regarding this practice.

Don't Recycle Sensitive Documents

This recommendation may go against good recycling habits but identity thieves are more likely to target documents containing confidential information such as a bank statement in a paper bin than in an all purpose trash bin. Therefore, if you must recycle, make sure you fully shred all important documents before discard.

Shred All Documents

Regardless of where you dispose of your documents, it's always a good habit to shred your important documents to pieces. When you lack a shredder, make sure you manually shred the documents with the help of a pair of scissors and dispose of them along with other trash to make the information even more difficult to retrieve.

Follow Up With Missed Statements

You probably receive periodic statements for your various accounts. These statements could be your credit card and other bank account statements. Make sure you notice when these documents do not arrive in your mailbox and follow up with the institution to make sure an authorized change of address was not made to divert mails. Sometimes fraudsters may divert your mails to another address in order to avoid getting detected when they commit fraud under your name.

Place Trash Cans for Pickup at Last Moment

The longer a trash can stays on public streets for pickup, the more vulnerable your information becomes to theft. Make sure you place your trash for pickup at the last possible moment to minimize theft. Dumpster diving is a serious threat and is commonly used to steal personal information from dumpsters.

Check Your Credit Reports

A periodic review of your credit reports can not only give you information about erroneously reported information to the credit reporting agencies but can also bring unauthorized transactions to your attention. You can also sign up for credit report alerts which warn you about any update to your reports which you should review to make sure they are valid transactions and changes. The frequency by which you should check your reports depends on whether you are using any automated alerts. If you receive automated alerts warning you of changes to your credit reports, I would say annual review of your reports is sufficient. However, if you do not receive credit report change alerts, then you should review them at least quarterly. You can buy your credit reports from Experian, Equifax or TransUnion, however, before you pay for copies of your credit reports, read the next tip on how to get yours for free.

Never Pay for Credit Reports

Current identity theft laws allow consumers to obtain FREE copies of their credit reports from each of the three credit bureaus every 12 months. However, most consumers do not know about this important law. Some companies claim to give away free credit reports while taking advantage of this law and selling more services to consumers. This item is so important to me that I felt I needed to bring it up more than once in this book. Please visit www.annualcreditreport.com to get a free copy of your credit report every 12 months from each of the three credit bureaus.

Always Review Your Statements

You should review your account statements even if you think you have no transactions or your balance is zero. For example, even when your credit card bills are paid in full and never used, you should not blindly consider your balance is zero and must review the details to detect unknown transactions.

Most of us tend to not review $0 balance statements. We just assume the balance is 0 and throw away the statement. However, it's strongly suggested to review the statement to validate the assumption because if we don't review, unauthorized transactions will go undetected allowing fraud to go on much longer, and our credit will be ruined because we failed to notify the institution on a timely basis or make the minimum payment until the case is resolved.

Consider Real Time Monitoring

Detecting fraud has many benefits however quick and timely detection proves to be even more beneficial. Although a careful review of monthly and other periodic statements will help detect fraud, the detection may be somewhat delayed. In addition to automated services which notify consumers of any changes made to their credit reports and other files for timely fraud detection, reviewing account balances and transactions daily is an extremely important practice for detecting fraud as it occurs. You should consider logging into your major online accounts daily and spending a few seconds to review the balance and possibly the latest transactions if the balance appears to be abnormal.

Another very useful method for real time account monitoring and fraud detection is activating the account change notification feature which is offered by most online banking systems. As you activate this feature, you will receive notifications (usually emails) when your account information is changed such as your deposits and withdrawals. Although you can select the criteria for which you want to be notified, there is a set of criteria established by banks which will automatically send you notifications when a major change occurs such as when an address or account pass code is changed.

Follow Up With Suspicious Transactions

After you review your statements and if you come across questionable transactions, don't delay contacting the bank assuming that they are innocent errors which will magically go away by themselves. It may be an indication of worse things to come especially if they are not dealt with immediately.

Under FACTA, You have the right to obtain documents related to fraudulent transactions or accounts opened using your personal information. If and when you come across a fraudulent transaction during the review of your credit reports, you can contact the creditors or the business owner of that transaction and ask in writing for documentation supporting the transaction.

Sign Up for Automated Services

This is a very important section to understand. First, you must know that you can obtain free copies of your credit reports, review changes to your personal records, and place fraud alerts on your credit reports YOURSELF. Second, you need to know that automated services alone can not fully and effectively protect your identity without your involvement; you still need to adjust your behavior AND review changes made to your personal records because an automated program will only warn you that a change was recorded in your credit report but can not know whether you authorized the change or not. Only you know what transactions you authorize.

That said, the best approach is to automate identity protection processes when available and where it makes the most sense time wise and budget wise. I personally use automated services to receive alerts regarding changes made to my credit reports and other personal records such as public records. When I receive an alert warning me of a change to my personal record, I review the change to make sure it was related to one of my own transactions.

When considering some identity protection automation, make sure you sign up for automated services where you need the most help, and where it makes the most sense to help you save time and money or remember an action such as renewing fraud alerts.

Create a Fraud Action Plan

When identity theft happens and you become a fraud victim, you should create a fraud action plan before you do any thing. Such plan will give you organized guidance and steps to fully document your actions, contact and report your case to the appropriate entities, limit and recover from fraud, and gain control of your life again.

Contact the Institution

When you come across unrecognized transactions in your existing accounts or credit reports, you must contact the institution to verify the transactions. Sometimes, when we don't recognize certain transactions or accounts, it may not be related to identity theft but rather a case of error or forgotten transaction. This is an important step because it will help you validate your assumptions and potentially save you time and give you immediate peace of mind.

Document Your Case

The Identity Theft Affidavit is a document developed by the Federal Trade Commission (FTC) to help victims of identity theft document the details of their case before contacting the appropriate banks and companies. Although this document is specifically developed to address fraudulent new accounts opened under victim's names, I believe it can also be used to document fraudulent transactions made on existing accounts. Although, this document is not required if a police report is obtained, it is still a good idea to document the details of the identity theft case including any witnesses to prove innocence.

File a Police Report

Some of the benefits of filing a police report include; blocking fraudulent information from appearing on the credit reports, preventing a company from continuing to collect or sell fraudulent debts to others for collection; and placing an extended fraud alert on the credit reports. It has been reported that identity theft cases are taken seriously by the police who issue identity theft reports as millions are affected every year, and such report is increasingly required by other parties for the benefits listed above.

Part Three:
Identity Theft Solutions

Chapter 13: *Detecting Identity Theft*

Credit report monitoring has become the main focus in the fight against identity theft and fraud detection. Although credit monitoring is a great way to detect signs of credit fraud such as unauthorized new credit accounts, credit line increases and change of address, credit monitoring is not a complete solution for managing identity theft but rather a component of a full cycle identity protection. The majority of identity protection services in the market today focus on selling credit reports followed by monitoring and fraud resolution services. Although I fully agree that we have to monitor our credit report activities to detect any unauthorized use of our identity, there are some limitations and rules associated with effective credit report monitoring for detecting fraud that we need to discuss. The high level rules and limitations include; a) credit report monitoring must be performed in a real time basis to be effective, b) credit report monitoring will not detect all fraud, and c) credit report changes must be reviewed and acted upon diligently.

First, to detect credit fraud on a timely basis, a credit monitoring process must be performed in real time. In other words, any unauthorized changes made to the credit reports must be reviewed and detected as soon as possible. Many people may just purchase a copy of their credit reports every six months or annually and review its contents; however, an infrequent and lengthy review interval will delay the detection process causing fraud to continue for much longer. Most often, consumers notice identity theft cases upon discovery of fraud either through monitoring their accounts or notification of various matters from the affected institutions. Therefore, any delayed fraud detection may lead to higher fraud costs and consequences.

Next, credit report monitoring will not help consumers detect other types of crimes such as the unauthorized use of existing accounts unless when consumers are contacted by various institutions for late payments or investigated activities and crimes. Also, if mails are illegally forwarded to some other place due to an unauthorized address change at the post office, the illegal act will not be reported in the credit report and detected through a review of the credit report or the missing account statements. As such, any delayed fraud detection may lead to increased liability for consumers as they are required to report fraud within a predefined period of time depending on the types of account fraud.

With regards to unauthorized activities inflicted upon existing accounts, consumers most likely will detect fraud when they review their account statements; however, fraud detection through the monthly or quarterly statement review will also be delayed allowing identity thieves to take maximum advantage of the targeted accounts. For a timely detection of credit card, credit line, checking or savings account fraud, consumers should review their account activities more frequently such as daily reviews of online account activities, or, on a real time basis by setting up an account activity notification system which most institutions offer by sending emails when a new transaction or change hits the account. This way, all activities are monitored as they occur to detect potential fraud as soon as possible.

Lastly, most consumers do not have the necessary skills to review and detect potential fraud reported in their credit reports. Effective credit fraud detection requires the necessary skills needed to not only understand the reported information in the credit reports but also to analyze and detect suspicious activities.

As businesses do their part for protecting consumer information within the boundaries of their business environment, consumer awareness and active involvement is also necessary to reduce identity theft outside the business boundaries as consumers continue to be targeted by identity thieves who rightfully conceive consumers to be the bridge to quick and easy identity fraud.

Consumers must learn all they can about the contents of credit reports, how to notice and detect signs of identity theft, and what to do after fraud is detected. Consumers should also sign up for automated credit report change notification services for timely fraud detection and other identity monitoring services to detect non credit related identity fraud. Every attempt must be made to effectively detect and address fraud in all areas of concern and as quickly as possible.

Chapter 14: *Getting Free Credit Reports*

If you are unable to automate your fraud detection efforts for quick containment and recovery, you should at least review your annual credit reports to detect and investigate potential credit fraud which may have affected your credit files. The good news is that consumers can now get free copies of their credit reports from all three credit reporting agencies every year.

With regards to new account fraud, the best way to find out if our identities are used to open unauthorized new accounts is to check the credit reports for any new information. One of the ways to quickly obtain such information is through an automated credit report change notification. There are many companies which offer such services to alert the account holders of changes in their credit files, public records or medical records as they occur. Once a change notification is received, online records can be accessed in order to review the changes and if unauthorized transactions are detected, they should be promptly investigated with the institutions. If you decide to forego the automated credit change notification service, you should consider reviewing your credit files on a periodic basis although the process can be time consuming and costly depending on how often you decide to purchase and review your credit reports. The most cost effective and minimum interval for reviewing credit reports is an annual review.

Due to the rise in identity theft cases and number of victims, the Fair and

Accurate Credit Transactions Act (FACTA) was implemented to establish and enforce certain business requirements and consumer rights which among other things state that consumers should be able to request and obtain a free credit report once every 12 months from each of the three nationwide consumer credit reporting agencies in order to review its information and detect fraud.

Consumers can obtain their free credit reports online if they have access to the Internet or by mail and phone. As a result of the FACTA creation and the need to comply with Federal laws, the *www. AnnualCreditReport.com* website was created by the three nationwide consumer credit reporting companies; Equifax, Experian and TransUnion, to allow consumers to centrally request free annual credit reports from all three agencies once every year.

The *www.AnnualCreditReport.com* website provides consumers with the secure means to print their credit reports from the Internet. If consumers don't have access to a computer or the Internet, they can also request their credit reports by calling 1-877-322-8228 which will take 15 days to process.

To request copies of free credit reports by mail which will also take 15 days to process, a form must be downloaded from www.annualcreditreport.com, completed and sent to:

Annual Credit Report Request Service
P.O. Box 105281
Atlanta, GA 30348-5281

Please notice that online requests for free credit reports are processed within minutes.

Chapter 15: *Life after Identity Theft*

As we have discussed throughout this book, identity theft is inevitable and will happen to you or someone you know in some way and form. When identity theft happens as a result of a security breach at a company, you might receive an identity theft notification letter from the company. The letter regretfully informs you that your personal information which you have shared as part of a business or medical transaction in the past, including your social security number, name, address, phone number and credit card numbers were compromised in a security breach by either internal company employees, external partiers or hackers who remotely penetrated the computer systems. The letter ends with "This identity theft notification is provided to allow you to take all necessary and precautionary steps to protect yourself against potential identity theft risks". After you're done reading this letter, how do you feel? Do you even care? And, what are you supposed to do?

Businesses are required to notify consumers within a reasonable time about their security breach incidents that have compromised the protection of customers' personal information. This is to allow customers to protect themselves against potential identity theft by any means at their disposals. Most large companies have a consumer notification procedure in place for such incidents to comply with the laws. An identity theft notification procedure is not only the law but should be considered as part of a good customer service and customer retention program.

Companies usually provide detailed information in their breach notification letters describing the case including how it happened, when it happened and what information was compromised. Companies notify their customers within a reasonable period after they discover the incident and assess the identity theft risks to their customers. After they explain the situation, companies also provide a plan of action that consumers could take to protect themselves. Some companies also provide financial support so that consumers can execute the plan without delay.

Consumers for their part should demand further clarifications from the company if they feel they need more information. They should follow the steps outlined in the identity theft notification letter and take advantage of the offer that the company might extend to its customers whose personal information were compromised. Sometimes, companies offer consumers free credit reports and monitoring services for a period of time (usually one year) to help consumers detect and report identity fraud which should not be overlooked by consumers. In such cases, consumers should be more vigilant and regularly review their accounts for a while and setup account activity alerts to detect fraud as it occurs.

Chapter 16: *Identity Theft Action Plan*

Risk management professionals can tell you that some risks can never be completely eliminated even when time and money may be available in unlimited quantities. Identity theft is not an exception and can happen to any one, although, you can reduce the risk of its occurrence and the extent of its damage by taking advantage of some of the recommendations in this book. When identity theft happens and you become a fraud victim, you should first create a roadmap to recovery before you take the first step. Such plan will give you organized guidance and steps to fully document your recovery progress and gain control of your life again.

As mentioned, putting a fraud action plan together is the first thing that needs to be done upon discovery of an identity fraud. The plan will be the roadmap to fraud identification, damage assessment, and recovery. The results of the action plan will depend on the completeness of the steps outlined in the plan and their effective execution. Although there are laws to protect consumers, a decisive and quick action on the part of consumers can reduce fraud liability including under the Electronic Fund Transfer Act or EFTA for all electronic banking transactions (ATM and debit cards) which is limited to $50 only when financial institution are notified within 2 days of fraud occurrence. From day 3 to day 60, the liability may be increased to $500, and after day 60, consumers may be liable for all charges. Consumers have generally more time and protection under the Fair Credit Billing Act or FCBA when they face credit card fraud.

What to include in a fraud action plan

A fraud action plan is a "to do" list, but also a tool to document the results of the actions taken. For example, depending on the specific case, the credit card company may be contacted, a copy of the credit report may be obtained, and the case may be reported to the authorities. During the course of the investigation, discussions with the various entities and individuals must be documented including the name of the company and the individuals contacted, their phone numbers, addresses, the date they were contacted, and any comments or agreements that were made during the course of the discussions. With regards to reporting identity theft cases to the appropriate parties, 3 main entities must at a minimum be contacted as follows and a copy of the report must be securely kept for future reference: 1) the creditor, 2) the Police, and 3) credit reporting agencies. In addition, the FTC may also be contacted for their information. Prompt communication is very important to initiate an investigation in order to stop the fraud as soon as possible and resolve any outstanding unauthorized transactions. In all fraud cases, the creditor must be contacted first to not only initiate the investigation but also to ascertain that fraud is the only possible explanation for the unauthorized transactions.

Chapter 17: *Dispute Letter*

We must formally file a dispute letter with the institution that sends us the account statements in order to properly refute an unknown transaction on a credit card or any other account. Some institutions which may send us account statements with transactions include banks, hospitals, colleges and universities, doctors and others. Once in a while, our account statements may disclose unidentified transactions, which may have appeared due to errors, merchant fraud, or identity theft. In cases where transactions and amounts are unknown to us, we must immediately contact the institution such as the bank that sent us the statement and refute the charges. Unidentified transactions are worrisome because they might indicate the beginning of much worse to come. That's why we must immediately investigate and attempt to understand the root cause of the unauthorized transaction. If the transaction is confirmed by the institution to not be an error, it is possible to assume that someone is using our personal information to commit identity fraud. We must put a stop to the fraudulent use of our accounts immediately and one good way to do so is to contact the institution and let them know about the situation. Most likely, the banks will recommend closing the accounts immediately. You must call the bank for immediate notification and you must also write to the bank just in case their systems crash and all the phone discussion notes that the customer service representative had entered into the system disappear. In order to create your own personalized dispute letter for unauthorized transactions, you can use the following section to create an account dispute letter for unauthorized transactions. You must make sure to use this as a blueprint and enter your own information to reflect your specific situation.

Date
Your Name
Your Address
Your City, State, Zip Code
Your Account Number
Name of Creditor
Billing Inquiries
Address
City, State, Zip Code

Dear Sir or Madam:

I am writing to dispute fraudulent transaction (s) on my account in the amount of $_____. Unless this is an error on your part or the merchant, I can confidently assume to be a victim of identity theft, because I did not initiate and approve the transaction (s). I am requesting that the transaction (s) be removed from my account and all finance and other charges related to the fraudulent transaction (s) be also credited. I would also like to request a revised account statement to ensure appropriate changes to my account have been accurately made. Enclosed are copies of my statement with fraudulent transaction (s) highlighted and my identity theft police report (if any) supporting my position. Please investigate this matter and remove the fraudulent transaction (s) as soon as possible.
Sincerely,
Your name
Enclosures: (List what you are enclosing.)

Disputer letter for incorrect amounts

It is also possible to discover transactions that we recognize, however, with an incorrect amount. For example, you may see a transaction for a restaurant that you recently visited but the statement amount seems higher than what you believe you authorized the restaurant to charge. Hopefully, you keep your customer copy of the receipt when you signed the credit card transaction in order to first verify your own assumption, but even if you don't, you must not worry and I'll explain why in a minute. If you have a copy of the signed credit card transaction and are able to provide a photocopy of the receipt to your credit card company when submitting the account dispute letter, you will allow the credit card company to immediately go after the merchant and credit your account. On the other hand, if you don't have a copy of the transaction, then the credit card company must follow up with the merchant and ask for the copy of your signed transaction. Although, merchants are required to keep a copy of each signed credit card transaction, not every merchant will be able to provide the transaction copy immediately, prolonging your account dispute process. This may not be a big deal to you since your account will be credited while your case is in dispute. Again, in order to create your own personalized dispute letter, you can scan or rewrite the following section to create an account dispute letter for erroneous transaction amounts. You must make sure to use this as a blueprint and enter your own information to reflect your specific situation.

Date
Your Name
Your Address
Your City, State, Zip Code
Your Account Number
Name of Creditor
Billing Inquiries
Address
City, State, Zip Code

Dear Sir or Madam:

I am writing to dispute an erroneous transaction on my account in the mount of $_____. The amount of the transaction posted to my account on mm/dd/yyyy for my dinner at XYZ restaurant was not $____ but rather $__. Please credit my account for $__, plus any finance or other related charges. I would also like to request a revised account statement to ensure appropriate changes to my account have been accurately made. Enclosed is a copy of my credit card charge slip from the XYZ restaurant and my statement with erroneous transaction and amount highlighted for your reference. Please make the corrections before my next payment due date.
Sincerely,
Your name
Enclosures: (charge slip and account statement)

Chapter 18: *Identity Theft Affidavit*

In order to properly dispute identity fraud charges which may have occurred as a result of identity theft, you need to be organized, gather and document all related information including any evidence or witnesses, act swiftly, contact all necessary authorities and companies which have been affected by the fraudulent charges, and promptly follow up to make sure that you do not become liable for any unauthorized charges made under your name as a result of your identity theft. You must gather and communicate all necessary and available information to each of the companies where either new accounts were opened in your name or transactions were posted on your existing accounts without your authorization. To ensure a complete documentation of identity fraud cases, a group of credit grantors, consumer advocates, and attorneys at the Federal Trade Commission (FTC) created a document called Identity Theft Affidavit. Although, the affidavit was mainly developed to document and communicate facts related to unauthorized new accounts opened under consumer names, the document can also be used to refute charges on existing accounts.

Although, the official Identity Theft Affidavit is accepted by many companies as the sole and only required document to communicate and refute unauthorized accounts and charges, some companies may not accept this document and may ask you to complete other proprietary forms and documents which is fine because the main purpose of the affidavit is to have the consumers collect and documents all the facts related to their cases and properly dispute identity fraud.

Another recommendation is to file a police report when you face identity theft. Although, the FTC suggests you may not need an identity theft affidavit to dispute identity fraud if you file a police report, I still think that using the document to collect and document your case is a good starting point even before you file a police report. A police report will allow you to block fraudulent information from appearing on your credit report, prevent a company from continuing to collect or sell fraudulent debts to others for collection; and place an extended fraud alert on your credit report.

Another benefit of an identity theft police report or affidavit is that such documents may be needed or even required by some companies in order to release to you information related to your identity theft case which you can use to further prove your case. One example is when you get a copy of the fraudulent application which was used to open a new account under your name to prove that the signature on the application is not yours.

A soft copy of the affidavit is available on the www.identity-theft-awareness.com website, or you can request a copy by sending me an email to henry@identity-theft-awareness.com.

Chapter 19: *Identity Theft Resources*

There are many resources to help you with identity theft prevention, detection and resolution. This book includes great and simplified tips to help you prevent, detect and resolve identity theft either through actions that you can take or some automation offered by third party service providers. Some of the identity protection services available in the market today have been mentioned in this book; however, there are hundreds of other services when you search the term "identity theft" on the Internet. Below are some major online resources to visit for more information when you need help with identity theft:

www.ftc.gov/bcp/edu/microsites/idtheft - This government website is a one-stop national resource to learn about the crime of identity theft. It provides detailed information to help you deter, detect, and defend against identity theft. On this site, consumers can learn how to avoid identity theft, learn what to do if their identity is stolen, and file their identity theft cases to the FTC. Businesses can learn how to help their customers deal with identity theft, as well as how to prevent problems in the first place. Law enforcement members can also access the information and learn how to help victims of identity theft.

www.identity-theft-awareness.com - This is a site that I created and continue to maintain which provides hundreds of free articles discussing identity theft for consumers and businesses. Some of the free features of the site include free monthly newsletter, news and commentaries, online tests, and soft copy download of the Identity Theft Affidavit and Fraud Dispute Letter. You can also use the contact form to send in your questions or comments.

www.privacyrights.org - Privacy Rights Clearinghouse (PRC) is a nonprofit consumer organization with a two-part mission: consumer information and consumer advocacy. It was established in 1992 and is based in San Diego, California. It is primarily grant-supported and serves individuals nationwide.

http://www.justice.gov/criminal/fraud/websites/idtheft.html - This website is established by the US Department of Justice to provide identity theft awareness and education for identity protection.

http://www.idtheftcenter.org - Identity Theft Resource Center® (ITRC) is a nonprofit, nationally respected organization dedicated exclusively to the understanding and prevention of identity theft. The ITRC provides victim and consumer support as well as public education. The ITRC also advises governmental agencies, legislators, law enforcement, and businesses about the evolving and growing problem of identity theft.

Conclusion

When attempting to protect yourself against identity theft, you need to create an actionable plan while considering your risks and the most appropriate solutions for your lifestyle. A major part of an effective identity protection is prevention followed by detection and resolution. Before you venture out and buy various identity protection services, take the time to cerate a comprehensive Identity Diet plan which will help you think about your unique identity theft risks and most appropriate solutions for you. In order to properly develop your Identity Diet plan, you must understand and take advantage of the Identity KAOS principles explained in Chapter 11 and best identity protection practices listed in Chapter 12.

As a society, we are accustomed to ignoring problems until they occur at which point the financial and mental costs outweigh the costs associated with their prevention. Many of the identity theft solutions offered in the market today focus on fraud detection and resolution services with a limited focus on prevention. For example, many companies offer automated credit report monitoring services to help consumers detect fraud. Although this solves part of the identity theft challenge, it is not a comprehensive solution. Consumers who sign up for credit monitoring services to receive email alerts when changes are made to their credit reports not only do not fully understand the usefulness and limitations of the services, but they also don't know what to do after they receive the alerts. This is mainly because consumers are not trained to effectively review the reported changes to detect potential fraud.

The Identity Diet program teaches consumers to consciously reduce their identity theft risks by identifying their vulnerabilities and incorporating best identity protection practices

I hope you can take advantage of this book and attempt to reduce your identity theft risks as much as possible. Just remember that identity theft can never be completely eliminated although we can minimize its occurrence and improve detection through planning and proper actions.

Please visit my identity theft blog (www.identity-theft-awareness.com) from time to time to read new and updated articles.

Be Identity Safe

Henry Bagdasarian

About the Author

Henry Bagdasarian is a certified leader in the fields of internal auditing, information security and fraud management. He graduated from the University of Illinois at Chicago with a BS degree in Accounting and his passion for auditing and risk management guided his career selection from the start and landed his first job as the Internal Auditor for a financial institution. After many years of internal audit management positions within large companies such as The Walt Disney Company and Fox Entertainment Group, Henry shifted his focus to information protection management and assumed leadership roles such as Chief Information Security Officer (CISO) and Chief Privacy Officer (CPO) within healthcare and financial industries where millions of consumer records are collected and maintained as part of the business operations..

As Henry pursued his passion for information protection, he concentrated his efforts on identity theft management and developed integrated and recognized identity protection services, industry terms, frameworks, and guidelines including Identity Obesity, Identity Diet™, and Identity KAOS™. Henry is the author of hundreds of identity theft related articles which are posted on his popular and free blog at www.identity-theft-awareness.com. His articles are read by thousands of global readers some of which have also been translated into other languages. Most recently, Henry founded the Identity Management Institute (IMI) to provide identity risk management training and certification to identity management professionals and created the Certified Identity Protection Advisor ™ (CIPA), and Certified Identity

Risk Manager ™ (CIRM) designations offered by IMI. Henry's identity protection websites include:

- Identity-Theft-Awareness.com
- BeIdentitySafe.com
- IdentityMate.com
- IdentityDiet.com
- Identity Management Institute (theIMI.org)

Henry was nominated for the Information Security Executive of The Year Award for three consecutive years in 2006, 2007 and 2008. He lives in Los Angeles with his wife Eileen and two children, Paulina and Daniel, where he continues to write, create new solutions, and provide identity theft management services to businesses and consumers.

www.ingramcontent.com/pod-product-compliance
Lightning Source LLC
Chambersburg PA
CBHW030356290526
45785CB00004B/1770